Poetry

From the Bottom of My Heart!

By Vincent R. Alexandria

Photography by Gerald Grimes

Graphics by Ulisa Lathon

Poetry From The Bottom of My Heart

Published by We Must X-L Publishing
Kansas City, Missouri

Copyright © Vincent R. Alexandria, April 2004

Printed in the United States of America
Cover by Lydell Jackson/Ulisa Lathon
Photography by Gerald Grimes

ISBN 0-9749564-2-2

special thanks

I have to give thanks to God Almighty for his works and blessings He has bestowed upon and within me. To my children; Randi, Preston, Royce, Azia, and Nia, you are the poetry and creativity within me and without your joy and laughter my life would not mean anything. I love you with all that I am.

To my parents and family, for all the love, support, laughter, and prayers that you all have shared for me, thank you. You have made my life rich and full of love.

For my best friend's in the world, Derrick, Gino, and John, you guys have had my back from the beginning and keep me spiritually grounded. Thanks for the 25 years of love and brotherhood.

I can't say enough to my ace-in-the-hole, Victor McGlothin, your friendship in undeniable and I would die for you my brother. Keep practicing on them bones and I'll let you win one day. (Smile) To my editor, Susan Malone, you bring out the best in me.

Thanks to all the great authors that have supported the Brother 2 Brother Literary Symposium. We are making a difference promoting reading and literacy in America, thanks for believing in the vision.

acknowledgements

They say a person is as good as the people that supports him and I want to thank all those who have supported me in my writing endeavors; Jeanette Lewis, Patricia Oliver, The Rev. & Mrs. Gary Jones, Mother Jones, Jimmy "Jet" Alexander, Bernice McFadden, M.C. Richardson, Women of Wisdom Book Club - San Antonio, St. Louis Church Family,& Fr. John, Marie Young, Frederick & Venetta Williams, Linda Martin, Candice, Travis Hunter, Jackson Mississippi Book Club, Zane, Women of Word Book Club, Lorrie Goings, Eric Pete, Linda Alexandria, Katie Wine, Aaron Johnson, Jr. II, Perry Alexandria, Donald Johnson, Frederick Williams, Lorrie Goings, William Cooper, Tracey Grant, Regina & Beverly, Emma Rodgers, Mosaic Books, Cynthia Guidry, Cheryl Shelvin, Kimberla Lawson Roby, John and Karen Ashford, Sr., C. Kelly Robinson, Parry Brown, Sara Freeman Smith, Nina Foxx, Jacquese Silvas, Brenda Thomas, Evelyn Palfrey, Blair Walker, Dionne Driver, Sean Tyler, 103.3 FM-KPRS and the Carter Broadcast family, Greg Love, Lady T, Tre' Michaels and 107.3 FM Radio Station, The KC Negro Baseball Museum-Bob Kendrick and Johnnie Lee, Arzelia Gates and the Gates family, Victoria Christopher Murray, Donald, Lillian, & Albert Dean (Cuz), Mom & Dad Ashford, Alvin Brooks, Mom & Granny Young, Uncle Pete, Bob O'Brian, Damon Smith, Elaine Dibartilo, Frances Latimer, Gerald Grimes-the greatest photographer in the world, Ulisa Latham, Sheila Goss, Sheila Shelvin, Ilyasah Shabazz, Delores Thornton, Michelle Chester, Nichole Poignord, Jamila Jagours, Katie Gibson, Kwame Alexander, Steve Perry, Lisa Cross, Lydell Jackson-the best artist in the world, Rosemary Kelly, Monica Miller, Dino Anderson, Omar Tyree, Patricia Haley, Peggy Hicks - the most spectacular friend and publicist in the world, Philena Wesley, PJ Jones, Quiana Williams, Renetta Davis, Cousins Verneal, Marilyn, Thelma, and Denita, Mary Jones, Pam & Rufus Williams, Steven Barnes, and to any others I forgot, I'm sorry! (Smile)

A Little While

A LITTLE WHILE

I thought about you today,
In a special kind of way,
I even heard the funny things you used to say,
And reminisced about your sexy walk and sway...

I dreamed about the way you move, groove, soothe,
And the way your loving touch makes my emotions
smooth,
Yeah, I thought about that thang,
So I gave you a rang,
Just to hear your sexy voice,
'Cause out of a million you're my choice,
'Cause I miss your kiss,
And the way you hold me with erotic bliss...
Oooh baby, I love and miss your style,
Do you think you can please, talk to me baby a little
while,
Yeah baby, Daddy thought so!

Black Pearl

BLACK PEARL

Diamonds are formed from coal and take their form from being pressured,
But a true woman is one who makes life seem pressure-less...

Rubies are red and are said to be kissed by fire, which makes it glow with
radiance,
But true friendship makes you glow from within and the only outside source of
that light is the spirit that is shared from that someone who is so uniquely close...

The beauty of precious stones lies within and true beauty is not developed,
shaped, cut, or extracted,
True pure beauty is grown from within. You are born with this classiness and
time develops its worth and rareness that makes it priceless...

The rarest of these grown gems is the black pearl; deep in color, bright in clarity,
rich in essence, and stands alone in perfectness...

I contend that you are My Black Pearl that I will always and forever cherish and
hold up high with chivalry and respect for the world to see just how magnificent
a gem you really are. Confident and independent, jazzy, classy, and
sophisticated in all respects, a woman well defined in loveliness...

Sexy, spiritual, humorous, and well read; not the typical woman in any sense,
will make sure that no one is mislead by the way you carry yourself, your self-
esteem, charm, and your full hip walk make any man swarm...

Your seductiveness, enchantment, mysteriousness, and elusiveness make the
brothers come correct in order to get exclusive,
The epitome of women and sisters in all the world,

I am so lucky to have you as My Black Pearl!

Chocolate Thoughts

CHOCOLATE THOUGHTS

Candied coated thoughts of your chocolate-colored skin,
Envelops my dream and penetrates within,
I seem to be all Butter fingers when I think of you,
Those cotton candy kisses and those voodoo things you do,
To be your Almond Joy is the thing I fantasize,
To hold you close and caress your body as I mesmerize you with my eyes,
You would be my Tootsie Pop and I'd give my tongue a flick,
As I tell you how many licks it takes to make it to that Tootsie Pop's stick,
I'd lotion you with honey and call you my sweet sticky thing,
And have you melt into me like apple butter when you hear me sing,
Deep velvet throated lyrics to seduce your chocolate soul,
I'd empty you on my bed and slowly lick the bowl,
You'd be my little Snicker candy bar and I'll make you smile a lot,
I'd tickle you with marshmallows, as I'd find your favorite spot,
You'd be my Peppermint Pattie and I'd be you Mr. Good bar,
You'd be my Milky Way and I'd be your Chocolate Star,
So excuse the little chase of this erotic candied fantasy,
With me covering you slowly in hot chocolate cream ecstasy,
I hope you understand that I fantasize what's behind that African shield,
And want to be that off-white teddy, and know just how you feel,
And cling close to your sexy body to feel your moisture and static,
Then have you moaning in pleasure as you call me, "Big Daddy",
So stay sweet my dear and don't even trip and I hope that you're not shocked,
At me expressing my fantasies and my sensual chocolate thoughts.

DADDY'S POEM

DADDY'S POEM

I sat to write you a poem today,
To write down all the loving things you did and the funny things you used to say…
I want the world to know what a loving father and man you were,
How you made me proud in all your life long endeavors…
How you didn't need a degree to be intelligent and smart,
How you were a man's man and loved with a big heart…
I wanted to tell the world how you would hug me in public without a care,
And how safe I felt just being there…
I remember the birthday parties and how we barbecued in the park,
The drive-in and eating popcorn to scary movies in the dark,
I remember how ice cream was your favorite treat and how you loved Mom from her head down to her feet…
I remember the importance of responsibility and how you withstood the racism and hostility,
You never backed down from anyone, but your faith in your fellow man helped you overcome…
I tried to write you a song today, but my voice wouldn't rise and I could not sing,
My memories filled my heart and it was a funny thing…
I finally realized I couldn't put you into words or prose,
You're much too big for that and heaven knows,
You asked for your roses while you were still alive,
'Cause you didn't want life to pass you by…
I keep our memories in my heart, mind, body, and soul,
And I give you my word to never let them go…
Daddy, I can't put you in a poem, because now I see,
That your entire life was poetry to me!

DELTAS ON MY MIND

A super sister walks by and sashays in her red dress,
Oh yeah, I was a mess caught in her intellectual, jazzy, sophisticated,
ladyness...

The way she held her head, with shoulders back and that confident smile,
Let me know at once, that she knew she was an African love child...

A queen in her own right, riding in on elephants mighty and great,
Demanding respect with her grace and in a room she radiates...

Eloquent with the spoken word, knowledge, and wisdom of the world; yet,
loving and warm,
Capturing the hearts of men with her beauty, sexiness, romance, and
charm...

You are my life, my dreams, my destiny, sun, moon, and even my stars,
An African replica of loveliness that can make the Nile river change
direction, is what you are...

So take flight in this love light, spread your wings, and let your positive
light shine,
As I sit back with my red jazzy thoughts of you and your jazzy ways,
Yeah baby, I got Deltas on my mind!

Gloria

GLORIA

Authority has always been your forte',
Whether it be at work, home, bedroom or at play,
Twenty-fives years of service and dedication you gave,
Now it's time to sit back and try to behave,
We all know that love is on your mind,
That muscle man with the tight behind,
Sixty-one and as sexy as a Fashion Fair model,
Sitting back relaxing reading a Vincent Alexandria detective novel,
Reminiscing about your friends at work,
As you travel the world, a sophisticated lady wearing those black pumps and
skirt,
Loving life and an intelligent joke,
Being lovable and just plain good folk,
You'll be missed for all that you've done,
And even though your retirement has begun,
Remember your friends still working their fingers to the bone,
As your man-friend treats you with chivalry and sits you on a deserving
romantic throne,
Let us know that you are doing alright,
Then put on that red dress and paint the town tonight.
So Happy Retirement from the housing authority staff and crew,
You beautiful, sexy, little Chic mama you!

I know

I KNOW!

I know that other men come at you facetiously and tell you how beautiful you are,
But that's not my style to impress you with my car; I'd rather do it with a genuine smile...

I know that people envy you for the way you carry yourself intellectually and professional,
But I admire a sister who can be so original, insightful and able to obtain her goals...

I know you get confused sometimes wondering who is real and who ain't,
But being the educated man that I am, I prefer to provoke thought and conversation about what a sister thinks...

If it seems that I may take things slow, flow, and be patient, it's because it is you who I want to get to know,
Have our feelings grow, eat popcorn and candy at the show or hold my hankie to your nose before you blow...

Could it be the sweet molasses color of your eyes that has me hypnotized or the touch of your skin, silky soft?
The thoughts of chocolate kisses dance in my head, provocatively remembering the things that you've said...

Do you think of me as the moon glows on your face and the stars shine their radiant light,
Do you hold your pillow close and think of me at night?

I night dream and daydream of the elusive lady, you,
If the same things happen to you, this is destiny and that would mean this is true...

To be in a room crowded with women all wanting to spend some time and space,
But I can't be moved to another with my thoughts transfixed on your lovely face...

You see they mean nothing and nothing they have I want,
Nothing materialistic can they provide or try to flaunt...

It's you that my intentions direct my heart and feeling to show,
And this is something I wanted you to know!

Now you know, what I know and I know you do,
That I know, that you know, that my feelings are true!

If I Could Hug You

IF I COULD HUG YOU

If I could hug for just a moment, all worries would melt away,
To caress your skin and kiss your lips and feel your body sway,
The pleasure and excitement that would chill my spine, mind and thoughts,
Would send me skyward as though I was an astronaut,
To hug you and see you smile and run my fingers through your hair,
To hold you close and look at you so beautifully standing there,
If I had one wish to make to make all my dreams come true,
It would be romantically dancing with you alone in the dark,
Kissing and hugging you.

If Walls Could Talk

IF WALLS COULD TALK

Lying here next to you
Trying to decide just what to do
I know we can't go on this way
'Cause if walls could talk
I would have left you yesterday

Verse 2
Girl, I've tried to understand
I've never been a doubting man
But baby on the other hand
You can be my ocean
And I will be your sand

CHORUS
I reminisce about your touch
Your smile
And your kiss
But baby if walls could talk
I would make one wish

BRIDGE
Loving you so tenderly
A special place for you and me
Loving each other in time and space
Fulfilling our destiny: eternally!

Is It

IS IT?

Is it the way you make me feel when I hear your voice?
Kind of tingly inside, full of surprise and anticipation,
Knowing you were thinking of me to call…
Is it the way I daydream about your face, smile, lips and eyes?
Remembering how I blushed when you walked away and spectacled
at the way you sashayed your curves so invitingly from side to side as
though your stride, glide and pride tantalized the material that
caressed your beautiful hips…
Is it the way my chest pumps, thumps and jumps when I hear you say
my name?
The way the words roll off your tongue with a voodoo taboo, daring
me to respond…
Is it the way I get caught in the potion of your motion? Like lotion
flows down the silken smooth skin of your legs and me in envy
wanting to take its place in your warm sensual palms as you slowly
massage it into your pores erotically…
Is it the scent of your body that casts the magical spell that makes me
receptive to your every word?
Or
The intelligence and caring in your conversation that attracts like
nectar to bees or fire to moths? Am I the fly caught in the spider's
web or the ship that sails in the storm through the jagged coral reef,
toward the saving grace of the lone beacon of light?
Is it the beginning?
Or
 Is it the end?
Is it?

ISABEL

Days were dark, cold, confusing, and dim,
My cup wasn't half full it was empty with nothing but air at the rim,
The light inside continued to glow,
But decisions to leave were slow,
But my angel lifted me, my self-esteem and spirit,
I got my stuff together and decided not another abusive night was to be spent,
I realized that I wasn't the problem or the monster in my dreams,
It was him in all his selfishness that was the reason for my silent screams,
I won't scream no more unless it's at the movies,
'Cause God and good friends are in my life to move me,
Move me through the hard times, but I know I got the strength to move on,
And with God, family, and my friends by my side, I won't be alone,
I remember how to laugh and have joy and a peace of mind,
My life is mine now, and it's about time,
So I lift my head high and face the morning sun,
And thank God once again that my life for the second time has begun.
I look into the mirror and I love what I see,
It's my own reflection, Hello Isabel, It's me.
I haven't seen that smile of confidence in awhile,
And I can see the love I have in the face of my beautiful child.
So no more pain for her or me in my lifetime,
I realize that these are the best years of my life and I'm in my prime.
So hello world, I'm large and in charge and without that abusive fella that I
know will live in his own hell,
It's me saying thanks God, your loving daughter, Isabel.

Mother

MOTHER

You are as beautiful as 100 star-filled nights,
You are aesthetic as a snow capped mountain,
You are as diverse as a rainbow, stretched across a waterfall,
The spirit of nature shines through your soul...

You heal with your touch,
Comfort with your embrace,
Give confidence with your smile,
And uplift with your glance...

You have the strength of knowledge,
The wisdom of intelligence,
The character of morality,
And the insight of ancestry...

You are more than a woman to me,
You are the fire of confidence,
The spirit of Christian living,
The glue that holds the family together,
And the fortitude that catapults your man to success...

You are the essence of love, faith, beauty, encouragement, village,
trust, and hope, like a rainbow after the storm...

You are more than a woman to me,
You are love eternally, perfect in every dimension,
You are more than a lady, surpassing the elegance of a dew kissed
rose, caressed by the sun, and blessed by the wind of your
ancestor...YOU ARE A MOTHER!

My Joy

MY JOY

The sister is fine as Nefertitti,
Almond eyes, caramel skin, with cherry-painted lips,
Her black dress is well fitted and a sight for sore eyes to see,
Her sashay walk is classy and accentuates her lovely hips,
Her personality mysterious, enchanting, and captivating,
Pulling you into her magical spell,
To hold her would be like heaven's embrace, so secure and mesmerizing,
Her touch would be like a resurrection, uplifting your soul from hell,
Her kiss would be like the ocean, abundant with waves of passion,
Her words would be your comfort, putting all your worries to rest,
In her mind she will be devoted, never ceasing to caress your ego's temptation,
Always letting the world know her man's the best,
Giving her love as she gives herself to you only, never trying to annoy,
That beautiful, magnificent woman, that I lovingly call, My JOY!

Playing The Shadows

PLAYING THE SHADOWS

Watching you sitting there so jazzy and intellectually,
Mind in thought creatively,
Absorbing your presence like a Bounty paper towel,
Not able to speak or mumble a vowel,
I stood there amazed, perplexed by your moment's gaze,
Your smile and the twinkle in your deep brown eyes had me amazed,
That made me so religious from that point on,
To marvel at God's most beautiful female creation, girl, you had me humming
gospel songs,
Amazing Grace and Take Me To The Water,
Baptize me in your love and thank God that your Mama and Daddy had such
a lovely daughter.

The moisture of your lips, the dimple in your smile,
Had me mesmerized, I must admit for quite awhile,
And this is intriguing, I've come to realize,
To see my feelings grow for someone so fast before my eyes,
To yearn to get to know you,
And don't care what I sacrifice,
To spend a moment, a minute, an hour's time in your life.

I'm feeling kind of bashful and embarrassed I have to say,
To admit that you've got this kind of raz-a-ma-taz on me this way,
But I ain't shame and really I don't care,
I have to be honest and let you know when my thoughts should be here, but
they are there.

Yes, thinking of you is a daily event,
And it's crazy that is where a lot of my time is spent,
Wanting to hold your hand, walk, talk, and make you laugh 'til you can't
breath,
Sitting by the water, sharing a glass of wine and enjoying the breeze,
But just like then, a gentleman is what I will be,
Playing the shadows, while your vision plays with me.

The Rose

THE ROSE

The fire of the red rose burns in your passion,
The dew from the morning kissed rose, slowly rolls down the small of
your back,
The texture of the rose petal is unsurpassed by the silky feel of your
warm, wet skin,
I am drunk with the nectar of your scent,
The passion of your gentle touch,
The beauty of your elegance, as your silhouette encompasses my body,
unselfishly giving myself,
Your legs the stem, that leads to your blossom,
Reaching for the morning stars, as I sing in harmony with the angels of
heaven,
My rose, my beauty, my life...

I am scorned by the thorns of your attitude,
Punctured and bleeding by your words, the crimson color of your
radiance,
Petals slowly falling, withering like your love for me,
Shriveling, un-loved, un-watered, un-attended,
Plucked from a garden facetiously,
To be used for selfish reasons,
Put in a broken vase,
With broken dreams and promises,
My circumstances turning brown in harmonious rhythm with leaves,
Yet, am I still a rose,
...Am I still beautiful?

My seeds will fall and I will blossom again,
Someone has picked me up and placed me in a book,
Seeing the beauty, for which I represent,
I am preserved, protected and respected,
I am loved,
For what truly romantic woman,
Can turn down the beauty of a rose?

SHAMEKA

Shameka

Shameka is in the kitchen cutting summer sausage for the Monday Night Football game party that her husband, Tyrone, just happened to fail to mention to her. Tyrone enters the kitchen.

"Shameka, I'm sorry baby, but I could have sworn that I told you the fellas were coming over tonight for the football game. I swear it won't happen again."

"It better not happen again. I've worked all day just like you and now you expect me to cater to you and your bum friends; and who in the hell ate my plum? I was saving that plum for me to eat, when I take my bath."

"I thought you didn't want it, so I ate it on my way to work. I'm sorry. That sucker was good though. It was juicy and sweet. Where did you get it? I'll go get you some more. I promise."

"Tyrone, that's not the point, I don't want more. I wanted that one, and I told you last night, that that plum was for me. You are so selfish; just like tonight. Not once did you consider what I wanted to do. It was just important for you to sit with your friends and watch silly football."

"Damn Shameka, stop trippin' over some stupid plum. I said I would get you another one. I could have went to the bar and watched the game, but I was trying to be considerate and watch the game at home, so you would not be trippin' on where I was."

"Oh, thank you *soooo* much for the consideration, while I'm fixin' the food for your stupid-ass football game. I wish you would have taken your tired ass and your bum friends down to the bar and left me here in peace. Now that *would* be considerate."

"Shameka stop BITCHIN!"

"Who you callin' a bitch?" Shameka asks, as she stops cutting the cheese and puts the sharp point of the knife at Tyrone's throat.

"Shameka, girl don't make me hurt you; put down that knife and stop playin'."

"Nah, Tyrone, I'm tired of you and your shit. This damn football game, your bum friends, you eating my sweet, juicy, plum and now you want to call me a bitch! I should cut your throat. Say it again. Go ahead and try me, *Tyrone!*"

"Girl, I ain't afraid of you. You better put that knife down, before I knock fire from your ass and I didn't call you no bitch! If I did, there definitely would be no misunderstanding of the pronunciation."

"Well go head and say it then punk, be Luther Vandross, and "Give me the reason."

Tyrone looks her deep in the eyes, scorched with anger. His face frowns up and he puffs out his chest. His face now red with hate. "BITCH!"

Shine

Shine

My faith in you has found a foundation sound and true,
My gray skies are now so misty blue,
Bubbling over with anticipation of beholding your grace, face and space,
But moderating my breathing and heart's pace,
Yearning to hold you close as we dance, glance and romance,
Taking a chance to fill time and space in our emotional and romantic circumstance,
Of two people in search of a joy that was missing within,
Slowly trusting each other's fate and becoming best of friends,
Caring about each other's wants, needs, and dreams,
Sharing an embrace as we watch a TV movie and share ice cream,
Not a moment goes by that you don't fill my mind,
Sharing your time and space as our fingers intertwine,
Listening to the pain that slowly dissipates from your troubled heart,
Radiating emotions that fill your passion and intimate desires that we both felt from the start,
Turning moments, to minutes and hours to days,
You can be my moonlight and I will be your sunrays...
Shining love upon you!

Silly

Silly!

I can't help the way you make me feel, although it's under control,

This anticipation I get when I hear your voice that strikes me deep within my soul,

Even though I'm embarrassed that you can make me feel this way,

I ask God why is he doing this to me and for strength I pray,

I don't look or say things to get a reaction or touch your emotions,

It's that I like for a person to know how I feel and I express it when I get the notion,

"Silly," is not even the word that describes what I feel about this circumstance,

Us both being married clings in my mind, yet at you I marvel when I take a glance,

And I think of how you'd feel in my arms,

If you'd melt by my kiss and embrace yourself in my charms,

And I'll understand if you shy away and because of my honesty, I'll take the blame,

And I know I should feel guilty, but I've searched my heart and I feel no shame.

I really hate that I express myself the way that I do, 'cause I know there's a chance in this friendship that I'll risk losing you,

But this chance I'll take and I know I'll heal with time,

'Cause I'll always have you to dance with, laugh, talk and kiss in my mind. Yes,

I understand that this is not what either of us is searching for,

And it's not that I don't have women knocking at my door,

It was something about that innocent time we shared,

It was one of the precious moments I'd spent with anyone and I liked it there.

So forgive me again, for my forwardness and prose that I use,

Blame it on my mind, not my heart and please excuse me and don't think that I am rude.

Special

Special

It seems that anticipation has always been a prerequisite for me, when it comes to you,
Noticing the smile on your face, your sexy attitude, and the jazzy things that you do,
I knew you were an intellectual by the way you held your posture, style and grace,
I anticipated you getting close to me as you stood in line at that special place,
I knew that when I touched your hand, my life would change right then,
But I touched it softly anyway and watched you laugh and grin,
You were confident and jovial, such an elusive lady,
And I knew you were a respectful woman, no room for slim-shady,
You asked me why you're special to me and to that, I don't know why,
But my heart and mind tell me you are and they've yet to tell me a lie,
So I trust in them as I trust in you and look for nothing, but what you want to share,
Just let me know and I'll take it from there,
So that's what I have to say and I hope it's plain and simple,
So that you can understand, so I won't make your water ripple,
I just want to be a fresh splash of water that awakens your sensuality,
I just want to share with you my creativity,
I hope I'm being up front and not to blunt for you Ms. Thing,
To put it simply,
In your life I want to be your Bling-Bling! (Smile)
So I hope you smile when you think of me and not be heckled,
You're beautiful, jazzy, intelligent and oh yeah,
You're Special!

Sometimes

Sometimes

Sometimes we can't see the forest for the trees,
Sometimes we get too confident to say please,
Our judgment is smeared by what we feel we don't deserve,
When we think someone is being straight, but find out they are on the curve,
Sometimes what we want can be right in our eyes,
But because of circumstances we fail to realize,
Someone that will treat us like a king,
Is lost in the between,
Brothers that don't respect you and treat you unfaithfully,
So many selfish reasons and to them you're nothing but a play thing,
But I see your worth and acknowledge your wisdom and intelligence,
And for that reason I will not play myself,
When you finally look in the mirror and see what I see,
Then you may want to get next to me,
So I'll stand back and give you your space,
Cause I respect you, your style and your grace,
I wish you smiles and laughter all the time,
And sometimes in my heart I wish you were mine,
I could show you what a woman should truly feel,
Joy, love, and give you devotion over load for real,
But for now, I'll just be a gentleman and kind,
And I'll sit and think of you sometimes.

Take You There

Take you there!

Captivated by your smile, style, and guile,
You had me wondering, even mesmerized for a while,
Taking in your golden brown, honey skin,
Had a brotha all warm and tingling within,
Yearning to get a moment of your time,
To kiss your lips and massage your spine,
To hold you close in the night sea breeze air,
To romantically take you there, I swear,
All the pain you've ever experienced would dissipate,
And I'd make you scream, "for goodness sake,"
You'd be placed on a throne of adoring affection,
As you notice our love dance in the mirror reflection,
To walk the beach and talk of things to come,
To sip on the shores, coke and rum,
I'd make you smile and laugh, as you've never done before,
And not one expectation, I would ignore,
I'd satisfy your dreams and put your mind at ease,
And you'd hold me close and my big arms and chest you'd squeeze,
And friend to you, I'd share my soul,
To be there for you would be my goal,
So make no mistake, when I say I'm charmed,
And there will be no need for you to be alarmed,
A gentleman and romantic is what I'll always be,
And you'd find that out, if you spend one evening with me.

Things

Things

Things will come your way that seem to just blow you away,
Is it life trying my desire, like a tree in the storm to see if I will sway?
I reach for my conviction and say a prayer to the Lord,
Contemplating suicide, to fall upon the blade of the sword,
But faith has taught me to face my fears and walk tall in adversity,
To reach within and find that place of tranquility,
For He has promised to take on all that I cannot handle,
And my enemies He has promised to dismantle,
So I fear not what the day has brought to my troubled heart,
I stand strong by my faith and deeds and will not be distraught,
For the rainbow is God's covenant with us and His promise,
And you are His sign, that I am truly blessed.
Thank you for your love!

Those Lips

THOSE LIPS

Those lips that accentuate your face,
Delectably sitting there, candy laced,
Glossed, painted, and plump,
Those lips that quiver and make my heart go thump,
Those lips that put the sunshine in your smile,
And radiates with charm as we walk together for a mile,
Those lips that I long to kiss,
And when I'm not with you make me yearn for and miss,
The sight of those smackable delights,
That can make my soul take flight,
Those lips that form and shape when you speak,
Those lips that you lick and I dream of when I sleep,
Those lips that curl down when you're not happy and your hair is nappy,
Those lips that when we make love, calls me pappy,
Yes, those divine things that I love to feel against my skin,
Those lips that make my love begin,
To formulate in a sensational way,
Those lips that I have the privilege to see each day.
So don't blush or try to be shy,
Bring those lips and kiss me you fool,
No need to ask why,
'Cause you know how I feel about you in my heart,
So let the serenade begin with those lips, you, and I in the dark,
Kissing those lips!

Thought

Thoughts

As the morning greeted you with warm rays of affection,
Did I cross your mind with sweet confessions?
Of how you might think it would be,
Waking up in my big arms next to me,
Or did you yawn, stretch, then rise,
Not giving one thought to my demise,
Did you wonder what I would do today?
If I would write you or what I would say,
It doesn't really matter, but it would be nice,
If I crossed your mind once or twice (smile).

Voodoo In You

Voodoo in you

It amazes me what you do,
This voodoo thing that has me tripping over you,
The raz-a-ma-taz that allures me to your jazzy ways,
Having me not want to spend moments, nor seconds and minutes with
you, but days,
I don't know how you put this vice-grip on my mind that has my thoughts
of you entwined,
But the sweetness of your enchanting smile and kiss accentuates my
thoughts, space and time,
So excuse me please if I might hold you somewhat tight,
It's just that those provocative thoughts of you that I get at night,
That makes me hold on and not want to grant your release,
It's the honey-almond back rub lotion that I massage on your body,
'cause I aim to please,
So I'll be your slave and devoted companion like a zombie in the night,
Making you orgasmically moan with romantic, erotic delight,
Doing all the things that fools do madly in love, so crazy,
Yearning, burning, learning your wants and needs and never being lazy,
Massaging your feet and kissing the palms of your hands too,
All of this, because of the Voodoo in you!

When Brothers Meet

WHEN BROTHERS MEET

When brothers meet, it is an exchange of souls,
The depth of intellectuality unfolds,
Speaking, seeking, tweaking plans,
Helping each other to understand,
Eye to eye and attentively listening,
Feeding on knowledge, wisdom, and beckoning,
The ancestors from our native land to clear our minds,
So dialog is processed and objectives agreed upon with shaken hands in
present time,
Respect for what each brings to the table,
Equipping each other and making us stable,
In careers we wish to pursue,
Pushing each other up in all things that we do.

When I'm 63

When I'm 63

I'll tell you a million times how much I love you and appreciate the way you take care of me,
I'll still kiss your wilted cheeks and your dentured smiling lips,
I'll help you to bed and warm you from the cold of the sheets,
I'll pick you flowers as we help each other walk in the park and we'll steal kisses behind the trees as
The young children tease these two old honeybees; still in love and feeling the arthritis stings in our Ben-Gay coated knees...

When I'm 63
You'll never have to worry about me, because I'll be by your side protecting you with the passion of my heart,
Even though you call me "An Old Fart" affectionately behind my back,
My love will sevenfold keep coming back for all the times you didn't know where I was and had been,
For 42 years I made it all up then, for being selfish and callous so to Europe we vacationed and then to Aspen,
Just to show you my love, thank you for loving me so deeply and devotion you shared when you pushed me to be,
The man the I shoulda, coulda, woulda been, I am nothing without you,
This I know to be true...

When I'm 63
I'll still wash your hair, rub your back and feet, make you laugh and hold you close until you fall asleep,
For you surpass all time, distance, and space, every time I look into your lovely face,
I'm reminded why I fell in love with you that October day at the restaurant at our favorite place.
You are my cherry blossom in bloom, filling all the rooms in my heart, making my world and existence full of grace,
Oh my God I thank thee again today, for my woman and her wrinkled skin, graying hair, but yet such a beautiful face,
And for this and all the love, romance, passion, I give thanks to you as I fall on one knee,
That you for this beautiful lady of 63...

You Are

You Are

Dark, lovely, and so well defined,
You make me drunk like an aged vintage wine,
Can I pour you in a cup and savor your sweet nectar,
Taste my lips as I look at your full hips and take you to the stars,
Yes baby, can I be your navigator...

Maybe sometimes just talk, listen, conversate on the way you perpetuate the spoken word,
Break down your sentences, conjunctions, participles, nouns, adverb, and verbs,
Can I get you to enlighten me to your chemistry and not to misinterpret your meaning or be demeaning can you help me see what you say as I read between your lines,
Would you please excuse, 'cause I would hate to be rude or crude but simply put, "baby you are just too, fine!"

Can I take this moment...I mean second...uh minute, oh damn baby; can I please just have an hour?
Can you be my flower and I be your rain shower, can you be the sweet and I be the sour in your candy lollipop?
If I'm going too far or rambling, it's 'cause you got me scrambling, to find the words to simply say that you are...

My morning, my afternoon, my evening, my twilight, my sun, moon and even my star,
Can I watch your lips and their every twitch, 'cause they captivate me and that's bizarre?
'Cause no one makes me trip, nor make my heartbeat skip, but you are the dip in my ice cream colored dreams,
I know this is long, but you are my song, well I'm really just saying that, Ms. Lady, You are my Queen.

You Know

You know?

You know it's love when things seem crazy outside,
Your head starts spinning and your mind is open wide,
Crazy cool feeling of green jealousy,
But you trust the person so you calm down and say it's okay,
You want the best for their mind, body and soul,
Even though your thoughts may be as black as coal,
Stealing thoughts of making love, laughing, and mellow conversations,
Understanding your long ride, in the dark night, cool and romantic, just right for mediation,
Contemplation of what the future may bring, wanting to run and scream, but loving to much to be mean,
I stand firm with arms open wide, not wanting to know what went on,
Mesmerized at the thought of him entering you sensually, hugging you and kissing you as I do,
Trust is a motherfucker, yet, I trust you. Am I a fool?
Yes, maybe I am, but it's cool, 'cause I'll be that fool for you,
And I wonder what you think when I'm at home at night,
You're probably feeling like me right now and I hope you can understand my plight,
Was this the beginning of your new future together or just for one night?
I have no right to question what you and your husband do,
I just hope I don't come out feeling stupid and looking like Winnie-the-Pooh,
Alone and blowing butterflies up in the air,
All by myself with you not there.
Well I hope you the best and that all the love you can handle is in your heart and mind,
And I know I'll have the memories of loving and kissing you, feeling softly on your beautiful behind.
I know you think I'm tripping and that's okay,
'Cause that's what crazy cool in love people do on an ordinary day, you know?

Coffee Colored Pain

Coffee Colored Pain

This quest to find the inner peace and
Strength in a woman that struggles through
Trials and tribulation, reveals a courage and
Tenacity as strong as any Colombian coffee...

To find the inner-love that lies within and brews to the point of a boil,
Stirs in each of us and manifests itself in courage, hope, and determination,
That moves us to reach for the joy and appreciation that we deserve, like a loving
back rub with jasmine oil...

Then we realize that we don't have to search for that someone,
That fills the romance, emotion, and love that we yearn and deserve,
That person has been in search for us and at fate's beckoning moment will bring
us together to fulfill our destiny and will listen to our every word...

So be yourself, strive for the sky, and let your feelings flow,
Because you are the most beautiful thing in the whole wide world and I wanted
you to know!

So when your pain is as black as coffee and you think that no one cares,
Look over your shoulder and begin to smile, because you know I'll be right
there...

Black Rain

Black Rain

Sitting in Baltimore in my hotel across from the inner harbor,
rain coming down as I watch and listen to Luther,
slow ballads play as my palate anticipates the taste of your skin,
as we dance in my mind over and over again...
The night sky is dark and the black rain hides the moon,
but that doesn't stop your glow that I wish to be in soon,
holding you close as stimulation, relaxation, imagination, and my
concentration focus on you...
Your sexy ways, your lonely days, sways in your hips as I dip you to
the climax of the song and you don't have a clue to what is wrong,
about the way that I feel or the things that you do to me,
can't you see, you're jazziness is killing me...
Killing me softly like butterflies wings and I sing 'cause it feels so
good, your soulful caramel-apple kisses tantalize me and baby if I
could, turn you as we two-step and watch you rotate as I hold your
hand, transfix my ecstasy and be your man...
Arms around your waste and no time I'd waste loving you slowly to
the beat of the rain making this dance, this romance, a beautiful
chance to be with you in Baltimore.

That Is Me

That is Me

People think they know me because I say "Hi" as I pass by,
Am I wrong for being the gentleman that I am and put women up on a
pedestal high?
Why do people perpetrate, deviate and conversate behind my back?
Is it just because I can begin and finish my goals and don't have a
tolerance to slack?
Is it me who is misunderstood or selfish, vain people that read?
Into my art of words what makes them feel good, sad or mad?
I don't apologize for what I write, because what I feel and what I feel is
what I am
And I can't apologize for that, Sir, Madame, or Ma'am...
If you could look beyond your inhibitions and open your mind, then
maybe you too could see that I am just kind...
But being blind is how some of us get by, painting pictures black with a
deviant mind,
Can only see as far as yourself, with a perception as small as an elf's...
I do not judge and accept people for who they are, and wish that everyone
could rise as far as the stars...
I celebrate life and life celebrates me, 'cause I can heal my scars that
people lavish against me,
With hate, envy and jealousy, you see,
That negative energy positively empowers me...
I keep my chest out and my head held high, I say a prayer and keep the
Lord by my side,
He is the One who helps me rise like the ocean's tide...
I spread my wings and have sight beyond sight,
My wisdom and knowledge gives me flight of light...
I touch a life with laughter, friendliness, words and maybe a song,
To know me, is to know that I intentionally do nothing wrong,
But mindful I am and mindful I'll always be,
Continuing to laugh, love, write, and communicate, for after all, that is
me!

What We did
or Didn't Do

What We Did or Didn't Do?

The night that we came to trust,
And refrain from burning, yearning lust,
I noticed how you watched me read poetry
And I was captivated by the way you got into me...

It seems my nights have turned to days,
The way that you make me feel has me amazed,
At how comfortable you feel in my arms
And how you achieved having me intertwined by your charm...

No one could have made me believe,
That I would willfully drive to you, consumed by the night sky and cool
fall breeze,
To race to your embrace
And gently dance with you and kiss your face,
Although the night ended with a tease...

I won't hesitate to come back to you,
And get another taste of the thing you do,
To embrace and sway with you by the light of the moon,
And feel my heart and head swoon,
And realize that our romance is in full bloom...

This is something that is not supposed to happen to me,
To trust and let you get next to me so easily,
And everything has me feeling brand new and I sense that what I feel is
true,
But we won't talk about what we did or didn't do!

What You Do!

I do not know what it is that you do to me,
You've got so close to me so easily,
This is something that I did not intend, or comprehend,
This thing that you do that you do has me so excited within...

Is it the loveliness you possess that has me tight in the chest?
Or the way we talk and conversate that has my mind in such a mess?
I anticipate your voice and the way you call my name,
I think of you often and how you've affected my dreams and have my
thoughts aflame...

It's funny you see, that thing you do to me,
I've had my guards up for a while, never wanting anyone close to see my
protected style,
But you're sneaky, sly and clever to get by my alarms, was that your
endeavor?
To be a cat burglar in the night, and have me in the aim of your sight?

Yes, I am charmed by your ways,
And have thought of you for days,
And I'm getting used to feeling happy this way,
What you do to me this day!

Spell

SPELL

Another day and no sign of my beautiful Joy,
The epiphany of elegance that I employ...
Keep me when I sleep and grace my dreams,
Please melt into me, like French vanilla ice cream...
Sweet and sticky thoughts of your honey-flavored memories,
Even though you are miles away and across the sea...
An anomaly to my very existence, stirring me within,
Eclipsing my world with your essence that has me contemplating and
premeditating sin,
What would it be like to hold you, kiss you, and open my soul?
Would it be warm as heaven or dark and cold?
Reality in phantasm and revelation in suspense,
Was our meeting inevitable or just circumstance?
Eruptions of positive energy flow across our conversations,
And it feels so good in all its sensual variations...
Contained feelings against the silent whispers can be heard from your presence,
Longing, yearning, burning inquisitions as you lay down to rest...
'Tis the confusion of this torment, that laments my soul,
Our ancestral bloodlines beyond our control,
For not this would our future be cast?
To know the fulfillment of loving, communication, and happiness at last...
To know the taste, smell, emotion, and touch of you in the very air you breathe,
To fulfill your every want, desire and need...
To concentrate on you when you are far and away,
To wait and hear from you on another day...
To enjoy your company and share in your dreams,
Being friends unselfishly will be a natural thing...
For your joy is my purpose and your wall being my conjunctive,
To say that you do not enlighten me would be intuitive...
I don't mean to get deep, unless it is deep into you,
So please excuse my prose, this mysticism is the spell you chose to do...
This is mythopoetic and I find it hard to believe that it's true,
That you could have this affect on me, but evidently you do!

Saxophone Kisses

Saxophone Kisses

Can I place you to my mouth like the reed on the mouthpiece of my saxophone?
Can I close my eyes and concentrate on you like the melody in my dreams that
Accentuate your every curve, move, groove, and soothe the stress of your day?
May I tickle your skin like the ivory keys that give depth and height to the notes on
my melody maker?
Would it be okay with you, if I blew every ounce of wind in my lungs by holding
your note?
Gently against my tongue?
Baby, can I blow your sound to the wind and let it echo from the mountains and
Scream love across every valley and sea?
It would be an accompaniment to you and me, instrumentally.

Can I dance, romance, take this chance, and enhance your Jazzy day in my own
little jazzy way?
Can I play for you?
Do you think that it would possibly be cool to undress you with my music?
Excuse me please as I fall to my knees like James Brown and let my saxophone cry
Like a child deprived of candy sweets,
Can I be like the Isley Brothers and get "Between the Sheets" of my music playing
Devotionally for you?
Ain't nobody home, so can I provocatively play my saxophone as you take a
shower,
Can I blow dry you with my horn and lotion you with my love notes as gently as an
Angel's wings and make you sing to my tunes of sensuality?
Ooooohhhhh Baaaabbbyyyyyy!

Play you say? Can I take you higher, like Sly and the Family Stone?
Get freaky like the horny horns of George Clinton's Funkadelic Band?
Can you call me "Mister Magic" like Grover Washington, Jr.?
Can I enter your ears, mind, time, and space, Baby can I enter YOU,
Like a Kirk Whalum song?
Ain't nobody home...
Just you and I alone with my jazzy saxophone.
Will you be my Missus and get all my saxophone kisses?

Romance

Romance

Yes, I notice the broken promises and dreams placed at your feet,
But I'm also aware it's a one-in-a-million chance that you and I would meet.
Place a billion chances in front of that at the chance that we would connect,
Excuse my forwardness as I interject,
The simple math and physics of this wonderful and spectacular
circumstance,
That would present itself and expose your craving for pure romance...

Romance you say? No, it's not what's in your physiology,
It's your beauty, style, intelligence, grace, confidence, and spirituality,
That's what romance is and that's what gets me excited,
Hearing your voice everyday, knowing you speculate about me and being
undecided...

You are caressed by music and your music caresses me day in and day out,
So I don't mind your distant gaze and your mischievous pout.
You are not something to conquer, but someone to behold,
Like a delicate flower that blossoms in the cold.
I can withstand your blizzard, snow and storms,
I won't shield myself from your winter flower and I'll embrace your thorns...

Being hurt can send us running with no particular place to hide,
I just want you to know when you stop running; you'll have a friend by your
side.
Holding you and embracing your pain,
I'll help lift you up and make you smile again...

You will owe me nothing, but what you are willing to share,
Back rubs, candles, conversation, and wine is what I'll use to take you there,
To open up those cold places that for so long you've left dark and bare,
We'll fix up that space and fill it full of laughter and love,
And you'll feel good knowing that you're always being thought of...

Friendship is what I offer and that is what I need,
Evidently it's what you seek and what your mind and heart want to concede,
I'll listen to your dreams, hopes and inspiration to perform and dance,
For this is what true friendship is and the definition of romance.

Can I Be Your Panties

Can I be your panties?
Pulled up slowly over your thick, just showered, tangerine-lotioned legs,
Raising like the temperature in my body with anticipation of
Embracing your essence, please don't make me beg...

Can I be your panties?
I ain't being facetious,
Can I be your satin silk, cotton, lace?
Baby, don't blush I'm serious...

Can I be your panties?
I would love your secrecy dry, moist, or wet,
I'll embrace your hips when you stand, walk, run, or sit,
You can smell me when I'm soft and hot out of the dryer,
You can read my poems and I'll embrace you when your secret garden is on
fire...

Can I be your panties?
It would be so cool being up under your tight-fitting dress,
Being pulled up and down, folded and pressed,
You can wear a different color to fit your mood,
Red when you're mad, blue when you're sad, black when you're mysterious,
Green when you're envious or olive when you have that nasty, sexy attitude.

Can I be your panties?
And caress your behind all day and all night?
I would just love that; it would just be out of sight,
And when the day is through and you watch the hot water in the bathtub swirl,
You can slowly take me off and give me a little twirl,
Then toss me to the floor where I'll happily lay,
Waiting to be your fresh clean panties, another day!

MASTURBATE

Ssssshhhh... Be still; be quiet, as I get into the mood,
In the darkness of the lone of the night as I take flight, concentrating on
you, your body, scent, disposition and attitude...
The candle has been lit as I start to get wet with your visualization,
The ecstasy of the stimulation, the act of penetration,
As I strum, drum and come with you on my mind.
So deep inside, all over and through me...
Making love to your vision and our destiny,
My climatically private affair, as I touch myself down there.
Your clover taking over my body and I swear,
You are all up in there.
Doing me, like I need to be done...
Hot, wet, breathless and erotic,
Right there, Baby, you got it...
That magic spot
Yeah, hit it right there allot,
As I squeeze to your tease and smile as you please my naughty thoughts,
My body trembles and my inner thighs pulsate,
As I smile so satisfied... coming for you,
As I masturbate.

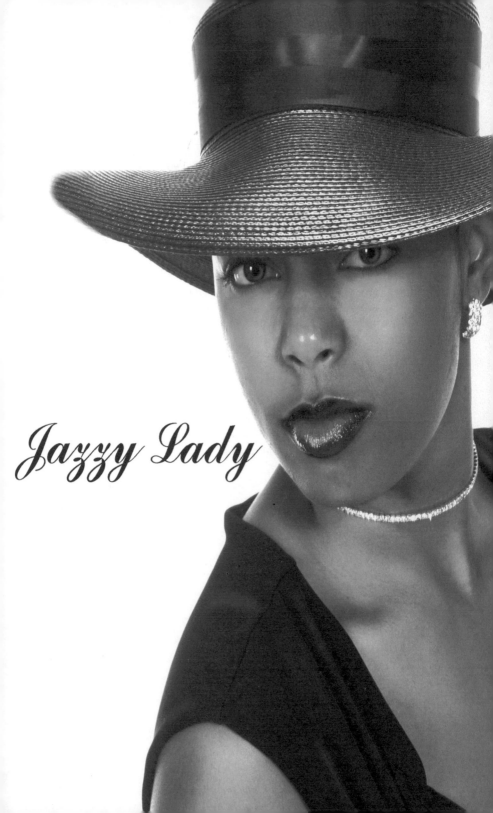

Jazzy Lady

Jazzy Lady

Walking around in your African wear,
Helplessly captivated I stare,
Wondering from whence you came,
Wanting to know your name,
Yes, the color you love,
The day you were born
And your favorite food,
Wanting to share your thoughts laughs and intimate moods.

What were you thinking and could I ease your concerns,
Make you laugh, listen to your dreams and share your drink is what I yearned,
Elusive lady, intelligence shown in your facial expression,
Confidence in your stride, pride in your strut, self-esteem,
And sense of self exhibited positive confessions of your jazzy perfection...
What are your jazzy dreams, seams and schemes?

Those beams from your jazzy eyes,
That hypnotize and make men cry,
Because they can't get next to you,
Make men feel so blue that
They are not worthy of jazzy you...

So you walk with jazzy grace, mesmerizing the place,
In search of that jazzy one who can make you smile
The one who's 'off the hook' who can make you look,
With the jazzy eyes of a sensual tease.
One who can please and make a jazzy one feel whole...
A jazzy kind of fellow, who is oh so mellow and has a jazzy way so cool,
One who can love your mind and be so kind and respect you being as jazzy as you are,
One you can love you near, love you close, and even love you from afar...
One who can fill your mind when you are sleep and embrace your thoughts when you're awake and give a thousand smiles per day,
One who can share your dreams and listen without solving your problems and take all your fears away...

The beauty is in you and all that you do and for your utmost wishes I pray,
That all you want is all you need and it's only a phone call away,
And may life be full and share its grace with you, Jazzy lady!!

Conversation Dance

Conversation Dance!

It's a beautiful thing to be able to sit and conversate,
To agree to disagree and form and intelligent debate,
To flirt, blush and listen to each other so attentively that the sound
of the voice fills our needs and such
To learn new and exciting things,
And the yearning to see your face that it brings,
To feel special and the flower of a person's desire,
To brush the heart with soft paint strokes and be the one that I admire,
So I take your hand and dance in my imagination, as I'm lost in concentration,
Twirling and moving to the rhythm of your voice, the tone of your pitch
And the image of your lips becoming moist,
As you imagine how we would feel in each other's arms, charms, and we
swarm
All the things that we don't say and keep at bay,
Until that one day,
That we dance to the romance of each other's voice.
Good night!

Desired

Desired

It seems there are times when you feel worthless, unattractive, and
unworthy of love,
Never realizing that you are the one that inspires my life, your
undeniable love is what I dream of...
Realizing what he can't see, my soul mate captivating me,
Although he didn't give you time, space, respect or romance,
I command my mind, body, essence to fulfill your needs every chance
I get...

To show you how much I appreciate your worth, mind, ladyness and
grace,
I'll spend quality time and alleviate your pain and put love in all your
abandoned space...
To see you smile and your mind be burden free,
To give you every breath, inch and width of me...

To fill your every wish, thought and desire,
Is it hard to believe that you're the one that I admire?
Desire, admire, inquire I must,
Can I get you to believe, conceive that I can achieve your trust?
To feel your kiss is the key to our destiny,
The desire you feel is the yearning deep inside of me,
I wonder why you can't see... My Desire?

Musical Dream

Musical Dream

"Betcha By Golly Wow"... yeah, as corny as it seems,
As I think of your hips and lips, that's the song of choice I sing...
With your Amazon hugs and Amazon ways,
Instead of wanting to conquer you, I submit to your gaze...

Big in beauty, like you're big on brains,
Your personality is funny, sexy, and jazzy which makes my feelings hard to
contain...
"So Amazing", yeah, Luther was thinking of you,
My sophisticated lady, my beautiful one, my boo!

"Mind Blowing Decisions" is a HeatWave song,
But if I could make love to you, I'll be like Lionel Ritchie and do it "All Night
Long"...

Baby, I'll be your music and you can be my melody,
Rhythmic, synchronized, harmonies playing felicitously...
Flowing together like a Brazilian Symphony,
Jamming, slamming, blamming our notes; yeah Baby, you and me...

"Happiness, together, it's love I guess I must confess,
Tenderness, your love I miss, its peacefulness..."
That's what I search inside your love,
Knowing we can fit together like hand in glove...

You don't have to sing to experience this thing I bring,
Just please come inside, my musical dream!

Four Diamonds

Four Diamonds

Four diamonds all gleaming with loveliness,
Each a different grade but none regress,
All cut from the finest and rarest stone,
Their mother the purest and beautiful stone,
All proud in dignity, grace and charm,
The light of the world, through which the prism transforms,
Aesthetic light that shines on all who see,
These four lovely in ebony totality.
Their heads held high and their smiles worn deep,
Each in her own respect can make the strongest man weep,
'Cause he'll yearn for her love and die for her embrace,
And her chocolate kisses will make him dissipate.
You can't take them for granted, nor put them under glass for display,
But behold them tenderly with respect each and every day,
So shine on ladies, with your regalities and sophistication,
Four diamonds secure in family, spirituality, love and jubilation!

To Blush

To Blush!

I blushed at your picture today,
The way you smiled crazy and looked so jazzy on that white chair that
you lay...
Remembering that poetic night we met,
Imagining holding you close, next to the river's edge at sunset...
Anticipating the moment I embrace you and romantically kiss your lips,
After taking I-70 and relaxing with you after my three-hour road trip...
I think about the way we laugh when we share our worlds, conversation
and thoughts,
I think of how I want to be there when you catch a cold, sneeze and
cough,
To rub your back, feet and massage your shoulders, to get deeper
In emotions and let our friendship get older...
To be completely trusting and sharing each other's dreams,
To sit at scary movies and have you hold me tight as you scream...
All this from a photograph and thoughts of teddy bears soft and plush,
And just form one night of conversation and joy has caused me to
blush!!!

Silhouettes

Silhouettes

Like air is to wind and wet to water,
Ocean spraying against the rocks,
That brings the sea in waves home to land.
Caressing, pulsating and splashing the cool waters
Against the warm shores,
Shadows leaving prints in the sand...
As we exotically dance to the rhythmic beat of our hearts,
Souls entwined like fingers to the climatic surge of the song in the
ballet of love land,
Dip, leap, touch, sashay, embrace, kiss, and suspend you in air
As the stars and moon in the night sky give ovation and
The breeze of the midnight wind salute the intimacy of the moment...

We dance the dance of love to the echoes of the seashore,
While deep inside my soul I set free the fire that burns,
Releasing the lonely torment...
Rejoicing in life, the union of love found,
Aesthetic memorization of untold desires released
In the symphony of harmonious movements that inspiringly astound...
Silhouettes!

Food For Thought

Food For Thought

I walk to the refrigerator for a midnight snack,
Home alone, and your loving is what I lack,
I open the door, and it radiates of you,
The coolness of the air and the sight of the honeydew...
Can I take a bite of your sweetness, like the cantaloupe I see?
And peel your clothes off, like this banana cream pie that beckons me?
Can I lick you slowly, like chocolate pudding from my spoon?
And dip, slip, and trip as you moan to the twilight moon...

Can I sip you slowly, like this lemon-flavored tea?
And toss you like this salad that is in front of me?
Can I be your cucumber, carrot, lettuce, and you be my salad dressing, fat-
free?
Laying on top of me and be that touch of flavor that I savor unconditionally.
Will you make me lick my fingers, 'cause you're "finger lickin' good"?
Or be "good to the last drop", like Maxwell House said you would?
Can you jiggle like Jell-O, or be silky smooth like a Moet wine,
Will you go down slow or go down just fine?

I contemplate as the coolness embraces my face,
It is not the food, but you, I want on my plate...
I close the door and lay down in my bed,
And replay the memories of our passionate love inside my head...
Food for thought and missing our recipes for sensuality,
Me pleasing you and you pleasing me!

Into You

Into You

I've never been into astrology,
Zodiac signs or planetary ideology,
But I'm into you...

You could be my black hole,
And entryway into lost galaxies,
Revealing the depth of space and the best parts of me,
Constellations unfold when you're next to me,
And it feels like Haley's Comet has penetrated me, you see,
I'm just into you...

I've never been into the mystical kind of thing,
Mythology, trigonometry or chemistry,
But I'm into you...

You educate me with your wisdom of who you want to be,
Where you're going, where you've been, and following life's destiny,
I sit back and observe your physiology,
Wonder why you sometimes use that women's psychology,
Trying to get me to do things romantically,
And connecting with you so spiritually,
Baptized in your waters provocatively,
Wet, getting into you...

Today can't go to fast enough to get me to tomorrow,
Another day closer to when we plan to meet,
Tossing and turning the sheets, covers, and you in my sleep,
Dreaming while I'm awake and sleeping in my dreams,
Wondering what is real or not as we do our sensual things,
Lotioning your body after a long restful bath,
And slowly massaging your feet as you ask me to make it last,
Pulling me to you slowly and falling deep into your hue,
Got me falling from the clouds and getting into you!

I'll be There

I'll Be There

It was your intelligence that excited me,
Not your beautiful physiology,
The way the truth and honesty flowed from your tongue,
And the way you looked at me is what got me sprung,
I'm caught in your web of curiosity,
Your essence has me thinking devilishly,
Wanting to devour your chocolate-almond body,
And dreaming of having you next to me...

A conversation of what truly turns you on,
The touch of a man, warm, witty, intelligent and strong,
But not afraid to let his feeling show,
By his chivalrous ways he lets his passion flow,
Into your arms and into your hidden desire,
That has a way to set your emotions on fire,
But don't worry baby, I'm a gentleman and I'll put out the flame,
But only when I hear you call my name,
Big Daddy this and Big Daddy that,
I'll have you purring like a pussycat...

I'll hold you close and stroke your fears away,
And make you want to be by my side everyday,
And you'll feel safe in the strength of my chest and arms,
And I'll fight to the death to keep you from harm,
I'll make you laugh like you never have before,
I don't have to try and be cool, cause I'm that and more,
I'll listen to your concerns and I'll be by your side,
And when trouble starts I won't let you run and hide,
We'll face it together until the rainbow comes,
You'll be my sunshine and I'll be your sun,
Cause this is the kind of man you truly need,
The kind that will let you be you and not have to concede,
To a Brotha that's selfish and unsure of himself,
I'll be the man that makes sure that all your needs are top shelf,
So this is the hope for a lasting communication of care,
And I want you to know if you need me, I'll be there.

JP

(For my nephew, John Perry Alexandria Jr.)

Thoughts of you with tears in my eyes,
Makes me come to realize,
The good times we had and the good times we shared,
And in your final moments I wish I was there,
To say I love you and that I wish it was me,
That was crossing over into eternity,
So you could have more time to shine here on earth,
But I know God had plans for you since birth,
To teach the angels how to smile like the sun,
And not how to walk to their dreams, but embrace them and run,
Some say your light has blown out, but it blazes in my heart,
And I know you'll be with me when times seem really dark,
So I smile at what you have achieved and pride fills my soul, heart and mind,
To have had a son like you so gentle and kind,
You touched so many with your music and grace,
And I know you're jammin' in heaven in your golden DJ place,
Keeping the angels dancing as they yell, JP!
I love you son, this is your Dad, John Perry.

Indecision

Indecision

Indecision, kind of like not knowing to say yes or no?
Procrastination seems to be the star of this show,
But I don't want to rush into anything, so we'll chill and take it slow...

Indecision, kind of like space without stars,
Kind of like red not being the color of Mars,
Kind of like mayonnaise without the jar...

Indecision makes me wonder if I'm paying dues for others mistakes,
Maybe it's feelings misplaced,
Or life without the knowledge of time and space...

Indecision is something a lot of people regret,
After having loss something that was dear, but what the heck,
Even if he did have you high on a pedestal and treated you with utmost respect...

Indecision is kind of like a person who can't make up their mind,
Kind of like a person being able to see acting blind,
Something like a mean person who pretends to be kind...

Indecision can make life pass you by,
Kind of like being depressed and feeling high,
Something that after the person's gone have you asking yourself why?

Indecision is like a hurricane without the wind,
It's like the Wheel of Fortune without the spin,
And like
Eve without sin...

Or maybe it's playing it safe and staying in your own little world,
Then finding out you've lost your black pearl,
That would have done anything for you girl...

Maybe it's you just done care,
That you really didn't appreciate having me there,
Or the smiles and fun we shared?
It could be the indecision itself that has you sacred,
By Indecisions!

Burn

Burn

I hope you like ice cream, strawberry or chocolate Haagan Daas is my choice,
And I know how to spoon it to your body and lick it off that is sure to make you moist,
Yes, you can grab my shoulders as I go to your favorite spot,
And make you tremble with joy, as your womanhood slowly and surely gets hot,
Did I say touch you all over, cause that is what I'd gently do?
I'd get into your mind, mystically, gently, and sweetly touching you,
Then I'd turn you over and kiss your voluptuous ass,
And start to massage your body from your toes to your head like nobody has,
Sucking your toes will be delightful as I play with them with the peppermint in my mouth,
Then I'd slowly rub my chest hair on your body East, West, North and South,
But I'm not finished yet, and the good part has only begun,
I'll turn you over and climb between your legs and have you totally sprung,
But baby don't worry about falling, I'd catch you and I'm not finished yet,
No, I won't be finished until your totally satisfied and wet,
Then we'll get to the good part, the part of our aphrodisiac dance,
When we'd sway our heated bodies to the erotic music of romance,
And then I'd let the cool waters of the shower bring you into my loving reality,
And you'll be secure in knowing that I took care of your sensuality,
And we'd kiss a little longer and talk about what happiness we have shared,
And we'll fall asleep in love having just taken each other there,
We'd meet again in our dreams and this time it would be your turn,
To embrace me with your desire fire, and return me safe without a burn.

Sink Or Swim

Sink or Swim

I never took to chasing waterfalls, those wasted moments liquefies before your eyes,
And the people that present them to you, you quickly become to despise,
I never grab for straws because I know my powerful grip would snap them in two,
But my gentle touch waits to embrace the beautiful one and that's you.

I don't feel like I'm chasing you, I've felt like you've been there all along,
Being the beat that's in my heart and the lyrics in my song,
I don't make rash decisions and I'm not an impulsive kind of guy,
And now that I'm falling in love with you it's no question I don't ask why,
I trust in what God have given me, what precious gift you are,
And I know that God has graced you with me, I'm your African star.

I trust in you completely and I will give you my very soul,
But I know that God has placed you in my life to make me complete and whole,
This feeling isn't sexual and that's how I know it's true,
What I eat, see, smell, taste, hear, and touch are all filled with nothing but you,
Sometimes love is hard and so difficult to simply try to explain,
My love for you is constant and to try to define it would be in vain.

So I give you my heart totally and trust in what you'll do,
I know that you will fill me with all the joy and love I need, because I believe in you,
Divine intervention brought you into my life,
And I know our roads has crossed so I can make my soul mate, my wife,
So give me all you have and let me embrace it with love,
We have been put together and graced with God's anointing from above,
And if by chance my soul to take and I do not wake tomorrow,
Know that I have experience love, so please don't grieve and be full of sorrow.

I've loved you a million times or more in my thoughts, dreams, and mind,
You have sanctified my very existence and baby you continue to shine,
For if love is not the answer and life is dark with despair,
Let everyone just look at us and our light of love will surely take them there,
To know that God is a blessing and He favors who favors Him,
I give my life to you sweetheart and I'll be there sink or swim.

Ms. Alexander

Ms. Alexander

Silhouette of beauty, shadowed in black lace,
In deep contemplation with an angel's face,
Eyes closed with tender thoughts of romance dancing within,
At peace with herself and confident with or without a man,
Elusive in the love that she shares,
Making any man want to be caught in her stare,
Chosen as her intelligent soul mate,
Making men tremble and anticipate,
The mysterious attraction and affection she posses,
And the touch of her silky smooth skin to caress,
A deep embrace and afrodisiatic kiss,
Would delve any man into a sensual bliss,
Can I be that shadow that holds you so close?
Touching your bare skin and loving you to the utmost?
Could I be your thoughts and lay across your dreams?
Can I be your honey, almonds, milk and peach cream?
Making you happy, warm and wet,
Or will I be the one you chose to forget?
Will you laugh at the slander as you drink Moet?
Or will I be your timepiece you chose not to set,
I won't mind as long as I'm near,
Your black laced body and I will not shed a tear,
Cause I know you'll come to appreciate,
The man I am and you won't hesitate,
When you get to know and feel the things that I feel and show,
Then you won't hesitate to open yourself and accept my glow,
It's your needs I'll fulfill and pamper,
The beauty and spirit of you, Ms. Alexander.

Angela's Eyes

What is this to my surprise?
As I glance at your presence and I surmise,
The encryption that invades your thoughts,
I believe it is you that penetrates my dreams and the romantic one
I've sought...

Contemplating your kiss, bliss, that and this,
Giving in to your every desire, fantasy and wish,
Reminiscing on our conversation and the touch of your thighs,
Falling deep into you and slowly being mesmerized...

Can I take a moment to take in your smell?
That's all it would take to be seduced by your enchanting spell,
Embracing your magnificent body and holding you close,
Yes, it is you that I need the most...

Can I make you happy in life, spirit, and love?
We both would fall on our knees and thank the heaven's above,
And I would be jubilant as I give praise and look to the skies,
Being lovingly captivated by Angela's eyes.

Abuse

ABUSE

It's the sense of vulnerability and not having control that has made me fear the dark. Yet, I feel content and safe not having to answer questions about the tragedy that has convicted me to be captive inside myself. I've been consciously awake for about three hours now. So far I've gathered that I am in St. Marks intensive care unit. I am in a COMA with severe lacerations to the head, which required forty-one stitches. I have sustained a black eye, a broken right forearm, my nose is broken, and I have two broken ribs and minor internal bleeding along with several body bruises. I feel the pain, but somehow it just doesn't matter anymore.

My name is Diane Smith. I'm twenty-seven years old and married. I can hear my husband breathing, sometimes he breaks down crying saying he loves me and he didn't mean to hurt me this way. I can feel the spittle and tear drops as he speaks over my face. DEAR GOD DON'T LET HIM TOUCH ME AGAIN! I scream, but nothing comes out of my mouth. I smell the scent of Cool Water, the cologne that I just bought him for Christmas. This smell is overtaken by the hospital smell of disinfectant as he returns to his seat. I've always hated that hospital smell. I sense his uneasiness as if the nurse who is now taking my pulse must be looking at him with disgust, his chair cushion squeaks with each uneasy gesture. "How could you love someone like this, you're a fool," she must be thinking.

My husband Lee wasn't always like this. I would have never thought he had a violent bone in his body. Lee was a very conservative account executive. He was handsome, physically fit, a self-motivator and one of the smartest executives with Opine Investment Company, where we met. We worked on the same team in the Auditing Department. We hit it off fine. Lee was my mentor and he taught me everything I needed to know about the company and more. This brother was also Denzel Washington fine and before I knew it, we were dating. Lee was everything that I had hoped to find in a Black Man. He was intelligent, well groomed; dressed straight out of Ebony Man Magazine; a gentleman and quite the romantic. I am a successful, educated, a former fashion model, professional and afro-centric. I am a positive, career-minded Black Woman on her way up, who knows what she wants and where she is going. We fell in love and were soon married.

Lee is the type of man that would take me out to fine restaurants, drive me home in our Mercedes LS Sedan, carry me up to the bedroom, place me on the bed, then light scented candles, turn on soft music, get a bottle of wine and pour us each a glass. He would ritualistically take off all his clothes as he danced to the soft music of Will Downey, Luther, Sade, or Anita Baker. He would walk over to me with his pecan-brown skinned, athletic, muscular body and kiss me slowly and passionately from head to toe. I liked the way he smells and feels to my touch. His wet warm saliva leaving gentle trails along my spine as my silk dress would fall from my body as well as panties. He'd pour Hershey's chocolate on my light caramel skin and deliciously lick it up, always pausing to let me share in the sweet, hot, cocoa taste of his kiss.

Oh God! The way he would grab my hips and cup my voluptuous ass with his strong hands when he would pick me up and we would make love up against the walls always turned me on. The way he would massage my shoulders and back with honey melon lotion and kiss my buttocks would have my womanhood getting so wet with conviction, I would shudder with desire. Once he got me to that point, he would sensuously delve his face between my legs and lose himself in my ecstasy, sending me to places that only he could send me and he'd be there lovingly holding me softly in his arms upon my climactic return. I was in sexual heaven and heaven's name was Lee or so I thought.

A year later our company was taken over by Trans-Continent Investors. Lee was next in line for a Senior Executive position, I was so proud of him! The President of this new company did not like Lee, because he wasn't an Uncle Tom. Lee worked twice as hard and brought the company a lot of money and clients, but this did not sway the feelings of Mr. Pen. My husband was loyal to the company and remained assertive in his ideas for future marketing plans, but the new President rejected each proposal Lee submitted and ended up giving me the Senior Executive spot.

When, Lee found out that he had been passed over for the job he became enraged, burst into Mr. Pen's office, grabbed him by the throat, cursed him out and quit. That night when I got home, Lee insisted that I turn in my resignation. I explained to Lee that it was his decision to quit the company and that I had no intentions of leaving the firm. I tried to reason with him explaining how he would benefit with my promotion. The financial bonus and salary increase of fifty thousand dollars would hold us over until he found another job.

Lee became furious. I'd never seen this side of him. I explained that we could work this thing out. I reminded him that I had worked very hard for a position like this and my life mattered too. I didn't agree with what had taken place at work, but what would both of use quitting solve. I tried to persuade him to just wait and cool off. Together we could talk to the President of the company and get his job back. That's when he grabbed me and said, "Bitch, I don't need you to go begging no White bastard for my job, that's just what 'they' want. I don't kiss nobodies ass, you understand!"

I told him he was hurting me and stop letting his pride stand in the way of our future. Quitting wasn't the answer. The only people he hurt were us. I explained to him that the only way to beat the 'system' was by playing within the rules and outthinking the oppressor. He slapped me and said I thought I knew it all and soon I wouldn't need him anymore. I backed away in shock that he would hit me.

He told me he felt that I would start dating the president of the company for giving me the promotion and that I was just prostituting myself to further my career. I started to cry and told him that was unfair. I was hurting so deeply and the anger just grew inside me that I couldn't think straight.

My head was spinning with confusion. How could this 'man' that I adored, think so little of me? Was this the love I deserved? I always told myself that a man only had one time to hit me and I knew it would be over. My Mama didn't raise no fool.

Well, two years and several beatings later, here I lay. The Doctors say they have done all they can do for me, that only my desire to live will see me through now. I guess you're asking yourself, "Why didn't she leave?" As silly as it sounds, LOVE, SEX, and FEAR. That's right, what kind of woman would I be if I deserted my man when he needed me?

That's the question he'd ask and somehow I bought into it. I just knew that he loved me and that he'd change once we got him back working again, everything would get back to normal, but it didn't. He could never hold a job because he was always checking up on me to see if I had any intentions of leaving him for another. Lee had lost his self-esteem; that which he was trying not to let the 'system' destroy occurred right before his eyes. I watched it all; he knew it and Lee couldn't live with that or my success. I decided at that point that I could not carry Lee anymore. I still loved him, but he did not love himself. I informed Lee that I was filing for a divorce, unless he would receive counseling and get his life and ours back on track. That's when the tragedy occurred.

Lee attacked me! I remember pain, scattered thoughts, dizziness, nausea and blood. I tried to crawl away, screaming for help when he grabbed the brass lamp off the oak wood end table, then there was darkness and I awoke; yet my body remained asleep.

I am a prisoner within; yet, I am free for the moment from abuse. How can you hurt the one you love. How could I have let it go this far, but I loved him so.

"Diane...Diane, Baby girl Mamma's here, everything is going to be all right baby girl, Mamma's Here!"

My Mother; Oh, how I just want to reach out and touch her, to hold her in my arms close to my breast to feel her warm embrace of love as only a Mother can give. In a way, she always knew this would happen. I love her so much. I feel her tears on my face, "NO-NO, please Momma, don't wipe them away." They felt so warm.

I hope no other woman will ever go through this. I hear my Mamma singing her favorite Gospel song, "Amazing Grace how sweet the sound..." Nobody can sing that song like Mamma can. Maybe I'm better off with the Lord! I'm so tired and hurt so bad. "Lord, I just want to rest in Mama's loving arms."

"Excuse me Ms. Smith; you fell asleep. That's a nasty bruise on your arm. The Doctor will see you now."

I realize that I fell asleep and must have been having a premonition. Lee grabbed me in a jealous fit and shoved me against the wall at our house. I grabbed my keys and left the house as fast as I could. The sex was great, but his love is bittersweet, changing as he has since he lost his job three days ago. "Thank you God for showing me the light of day," I prayed as I entered the doctor's office.

Midnight

Erotica

The Light Of Day

THE LIGHT OF DAY

Light is defined as something that provides information or clarification, spiritual awareness, a state of understanding, such as a light of experience or an awakening. My name is Diane Smith. I'm twenty_seven years old and have been married for three years. I am a successful, educated, professional, Afro-centric, former fashion model. I am a positive career_minded Black woman on her way up. I thought I always knew what I wanted and where I was going.

Lee is my husband. He was my mentor and he taught me everything I needed to know about the Opine Investment Company and more. I was naturally attracted to Lee because he had everything going for him and from what I could gather he was single; yet he showed little interest in me personally. I thought he was kind and he was always about the business. This brother was also Denzel Washington fine. Lee was a self_motivator and one of the smartest executives with Opine Investment Company.

Lee and I worked on the same team in the Auditing Department and we hit it off fine right from the start. We would have audits that lasted late into the evening. We would order food to be delivered to the office and during our dinner break we shared bits of our lives with each other. Lee had a spacious office with a huge, deep hazel oak desk and a nineteenth floor, bay window view of the downtown Kansas City, Missouri skyline and river. There was an eighteenth century Victorian, black leather couch next to the frame of that majestic view of the city and I would often dream of how that plush leather would feel beneath my naked ski On occasion I would wear my thong just to get a feel of the texture of expensive leather cradling my ass, as I lifted the back of my dress when Lee wasn't looking. Lee didn't know why I always gravitated to that couch, but sometimes I think he had his suspicions.

I had been with the company about eight months the first time Lee and I made love. were working on the now defunct, LeRon Pharmaceuticals account. We had eaten Chine food earlier and Lee had a bottle of red wine that was given to him by one of his clients. pulled it down from its place on the bookshelf, opened it and we both drank from the bottle recall Lee loosening his tie and taking off his jacket. I saw the bulges in his shirt created the muscles that rippled in his arms and chest, and I became instantly aroused. I wanted touch each crease of his body and taste the wine remnants on his thick lips. My pussy beg to pulsate and I could feel the moisture between my legs wetting the cotton lining of thong.

I ran my hand through my long black hair, crossed my legs tight and tried to gather mys and get control of my mischievous thoughts. Lee was preoccupied running figures at his d as I got up and walked around the office inconspicuously looking over files of the work had completed that night. I eased my way to the door and locked it, so as not to be disturb by the night janitor.

I turned off the lights to the office, leaving only the desk lamp illuminated that Lee had on his desk.

"What are you doing over there, Diane?" Lee asked a little disturbed.

In the mysterious glow of moonlight, I moved in the shadows back to the couch. "I just need to rest my eyes for a moment from the light. We've been at this for ten hours straight." I replied, as Lee shrugged his shoulders and went back to the task of auditing numbers.

I slowly unbuttoned my blouse and slipped out of my bra, leaving my full, firm breasts exposed. It's times like these when I'm glad I've been meticulous about my health and shape of my body. My nipples are already beginning to firm at my devious temptations as I spin my web of erotic stimulation. I eased out of my business skirt and decided to let Lee have the pleasure of unwrapping my sensuous gift of hairy vagina from my thong.

I couldn't resist the throbbing that was calling to me from between my legs and sent my fingers to quiet the anticipation as I bit my bottom lip, not wanting to be exposed too soon.

"Lee, can you come over here and help me for a moment please," I asked provocatively.

Lee rose slowly, stretched his arms and shoulders from side to side. He put his pen on the books, probably to mark his spot on the page, came out of the light and stood before me. It took a second or two for his eyes to adjust to the darkness, but when it did there was no denying that he had taken me in. The bulge in his pants expressed what he hadn't in the last eight months.

I stood and kissed Lee with the force of a hurricane wind. He put his arms around me. His hands caressed my skin under my shirt, and then went to my breasts and nipples, which were soon consumed by his mouth. I unbuttoned Lee's shirt and pulled it off, tossing it to the floor. I pulled his T-shirt from his waist and reached for his belt buckle, which snapped freely. I unbuttoned his pants and they collapsed to the floor. I just loved his baggy pants, "snap, zip, and drop. Easy access baby."

I slowly fell to my knees, kissing his hairy chest and stomach along the way, only stopping to let my hot tongue circle his belly button. I felt his rock hard penis beneath my chin, poking me through his silk boxer shorts. I rested my hand on his penis and felt the blood rushing within to make it throb. I pulled his underwear slowly down his long brown hairy legs. I gripped his manhood to determine its dimensions and I was not disappointed. His penis was long, thick, and even larger than I had imagined. It was so hard. I took it in my hands and began to pump it slowly up and down. He was caressing my head and running his fingers through my hair as his waist began to sway back and forth.

I licked the head of his shaft as he trembled with excitement. I sucked on his hardness, taking it deep in my throat and rotated my tongue around his swelled penis as I extracted it from my mouth just long enough to look at the satisfaction on his face. He had a childish smile of pleasure. I wanted to teach him that he wasn't a child, so I took him back into my hot waiting mouth and sucked on it faster and harder, squeezing it with both hands until he tensed up and his penis erupted his hot white cream all over my chest. I shuddered with excitement and let out a small laugh.

"I hope you're okay and glad you missed my face." I teased.

Lee took off his T-shirt and wiped the cream from my chest and sat me on the Victorian couch of my desire and gently spread my legs wide with his big firm hands. "Diane, let me show you what I've been dreaming about doing to you since the first day I laid eyes on your beautiful self." Lee said, as he slipped his face between my legs. With his fingers he slid my thong to the side and tasted my joy. Licking his lips he brought my legs together as he pulled my thong over my legs.

Lee started to kiss and massage my feet as he worked his way up my thighs. Lee helped me up and placed me in a kneeling position on the couch, crawled between my legs with his back against the couch. I straddled his face and would occasionally look back and see his dick standing at full attention. I let my hips fall upon his chin as he licked, sucked, nibbled and blew into my beautiful place sending joy all through my body.

He concentrated his tongue on my clit and I could have sworn he was writing the alphabet on my vagina with his tongue. I began rotating my hips in time with his motions. He slid one finger into my cunt and the other up my ass. I moaned with excitement. I had never had this done before and it was erotically exhilarating. I was completely soaked from my own juices as I climaxed on Lee's face and chin.

Lee got up and grabbed the T-shirt he had wiped me with and did the same to his face and chin. "Well, I see I struck oil," Lee teased.

I lay on the couch and pulled Lee on top of me, "There's more oil where that came from baby."

I grabbed Lee's erect penis and slid it up and down along my slit and placed it into my wet, yearning pussy. We fucked that way for twenty minutes. We walked over to his desk that was exposed to the moonlight, Kansas City's skyline and stars. I placed my palms down flat on the front of Lee's desk as he rubbed my ass, separated my legs and entered me from behind.

Lee kissed my neck and back and cupped my throbbing tits. He pinched my nipples and played with them with his fingers as I pushed back with my body and moaned with pleasure, letting his huge, black penis engulf my waiting wet vagina. I pushed back so that he was deeper and deeper inside of me. I screamed his name and moaned as he rode my pussy past midnight slowly and steadily. I loved every minute of it.

I wanted more, I pulled away and pushed all of the papers on the desk unto the floor. Lee picked me up and placed me on his oak desk and slammed his thick penis between my legs. He began to pump harder and harder. I grabbed his waist with my legs and clenched his firm black ass as I pulled him deeper inside me, feeling my orgasm climbing to its brink of fulfillment.

"Oh shit, Lee, I'm coming, I'm coming!" I screamed.

Lee pounded me harder and faster, "Whose pussy is this, Diane? Whose pussy is this? Lee panted and asked.

"Yours, Lee! This pussy is yours, baby. Whenever you want it. You are the mother fucking man!" I yelled out as I climaxed and shuddered as I felt my vagina being filled with Lee's climactic cream.

We lay there on that desk for an hour catching our breath. We hugged, kissed, and embraced each other watching the traffic lights on the distant freeway. We finally got up, straightened the office, dressed and went to my place where we showered and loved the rest of the night. Lee and I had a fabulous relationship and before long we were seeing each other everyday. He filled my every desire. We fell in love with time and nine months later we were married in Mexico.

Lee is the type of man that would take me out to fine restaurants, drive me home in our Mercedes LS Sedan with his hand in my panties teasing my emotions and wetting my desires. He would carry me into the new home we had built and up to our spacious bedroom. We had wood floors and two walk-in closets, a study off to the left of the room and a deck on the right. It faced a wooded area behind the house. Lee placed me on the bed and opened the French doors to the deck. The night breeze blew in the enchantment of the jasmine, pine, and chestnut scents that the wooded area provided. He would light candles, turn on soft music, get a bottle of aged wine and pour us each a glass. Then Lee would ritualistically take off all his clothes as he danced to the soft music of Will Downey, Luther,

135

Sade, or Anita Baker. His nude, pecan brown skin covered, muscular body would glide over and he would kiss me slowly and passionately from head to toe. I loved the way he smelled and felt to my touch. His wet warm saliva leaving gentle trails along my spine as my outfit fell from my body along with my silk panties. He'd pour Hershey's chocolate on my light caramel skin and deliciously lick it up, always pausing to let me share in the sweet, hot, cocoa taste of his kisses.

Oh God! The way he would grab my hips and cup my voluptuous ass with his strong hands when he picked me up and we made love against the walls. That always turned me on! The way he massaged my shoulders and back with honey melon lotion and kissed my buttocks would have my womanhood getting so wet with conviction, I would get goose pimples of desire. Once he got me to that point, he would sensuously delve his face between my legs and lose himself in my ecstasy, sending me to places that only he could send me and he would be there lovingly holding me softly in his arms upon my climactic return. I was in sexual heaven and heaven's name was Lee, or so I thought.

About a year later our company was taken over by Trans_Continent Investors. Lee was next in line for a Senior Executive position, I was so proud of him! The President of this new company did not like Lee, because Lee complained about some accounting deficiencies. Lee worked twice as hard and brought the company a lot of money and clients, but this did not sway the feelings of Mr. Porter. My husband was loyal to the company and remained assertive in his ideas for future marketing plans. He told me he thought the company was keeping separate books and that he was suspicious of some overseas accounts. Lee was meticulous about his work and took pride in accounting for every cent of his client's monies. Lee had some great ideas but the new President rejected each proposal Lee submitted and ended up giving me the Senior Executive spot. When, Lee found out that he had been passed over for the job he became enraged, burst into Mr. Porter's office, grabbed him by the throat, cursed him out and quit.

That same night when I got home, I found Lee sitting in the living room. Lee insisted that I turn in my resignation. He said something shady was going on in the company and he had proof.

"Diane, I expect you to quit tomorrow. We will find another company to work for or we can try and start our own company. We got a client list." Lee demanded.

I explained," It was your decision to quit the company. I like what I do and this is the opportunity of a lifetime for me. I have no intentions of leaving the firm. I will help you if you want to start your own company, but that's not what I want right now. Besides, we can't afford to both quit, we have bills to pay, Lee."

Lee was agitated. He paced the floor and I could see he was getting upset. "Look woman, either you're for me or you're against me. My job abandoned me, now you. What the fuck is that about?"

"The financial bonus and salary increase of fifty thousand dollars will hold us over until you find another job. That's the best I can do. We will both benefit from this promotion, Lee. Just try to understand." I reasoned, trying desperately to be supportive.

"Diane, I want you to quit that racist place and I mean it!" Lee was becoming furious. I'd never seen this side of him.

"Lee, we can work this out. What I feel matters too, baby. I have worked very hard for position like this. I don't agree with what has happened at work, but what would both of us quitting solve? Please, just wait and cool off. Together we can talk to the President of the company and get your job back," I said softly as I placed my hand on his back for support. That's when he grabbed me.

"Woman, I don't need you to go begging no White bastard for my job, that's just what 'they' want. I don't kiss nobody's ass, you understand. They're going down for what they did to me and I don't want you to get caught up!"

I tried to remain calm despite this desperate situation I was in. This was not like Lee. "You're being paranoid. Stop letting your pride stand in the way of our future. Quitting isn't the answer. The only people you're hurting is us," I explained. "Lee, the only way to beat the 'system' is by playing within the rules and out_thinking the person who's denying you your rightful position."

138

"Oh, now you're so fucking smart since you got my job? You think you know it all now!

Shit, it probably won't be long before you won't need me anymore. Well remember who taught you what you know. You're not better than me Diane, so don't start talking down to me, hear!" Lee demanded.

"I never said or thought any of that, Lee. Why are you saying these things?" I replied, but Lee wasn't listening. He just stared at me with a desperate expression on his face and I didn't know what else to say.

"Baby, I'm sorry. I have to do what I have to. I love you and you're right, Diane, but I've got to get out of here?" He said as he headed up the stairs.

I started to cry. "Lee, what are you going to do?" I felt desperate and I felt in my heart that he was about to leave me. So much anger grew inside me that I couldn't think straight. Tears burned my eyes and my head was spinning with confusion. How could this 'man' that I adore even consider leaving me?

I ran upstairs to our bedroom and he was placing suits in a suit bag and a duffle bag is already packed and laying on the floor.

"Lee, you don't have to do this. Where are you going?" I ask as my stomach turns flip-flops and bile burns my throat.

"Diane, there is enough money in our savings to pay the bills. I'm going to do something that I should have done a long time ago. I don't want to get you involved if this goes bad. Trust me, baby. You know I love you and I don't want to hurt you. I have pride and I don't want to bring you down. Just give me some time to get some things together."

Feeling like I'm hyperventilating, I sit on the bed. I try to speak but nothing comes out. Lee kisses me on the forehead and walks out of the room and leaves the house. I gather my rattled nerves and get down to the front door in time to see the taillights of the car fade into the night. Has Lee left me forever? What is it that he has on the company that would drive him to quit and walk out on our home, our love and me?

I slowly climb the stairs with tears rolling down my face. Sitting on the bed that we have loved on so many nights, I grab his pillow and breath in deeply his sent. "He'll come back in a couple of hours after he cools off," I tell my self, as I hold his pillow close and cry my self to sleep.

I wake up the following morning to find that Lee has not come home. I pulled myself out of bed and made a few calls searching for him, but none of our friends or family has heard a word from him. I get in the shower and dress for work. "Surely he'll get in touch with me there," I prayed.

I found it strange that there was a message for me to report the president's office when I arrived at work. Placing my briefcase next to my desk, I straightened my clothes and tried as best I could not to show that my world had been turned upside down. "What could Mr. Porter want with me? I've never met with him before noon." I think to myself and continue adjusting my business suit as I walk down the long blue-carpeted corridor and button another notch on my blouse so as not to show much cleavage. I never want to give a boss the wrong impression because I have no intentions of sleeping my way to the top of an organization. I knock twice on the big oak door to Mr. Porter's office and he says, "Come in." Mr. Porter is a five and a half foot, silver-haired, balding, pot-bellied man with age spots, and looks to be in his late fifties. He has a curious smile and sneaky demeanor. Mr. Porter rises when I enter his office and says, "Thanks for coming in, Diane.

Let me close the door. Please have a seat." I take the offered seat and Mr. Porter walks up behind me and places his hands firmly on my shoulders. "Diane, I was wondering how Lee was doing. I'm really sorry things happened the way they did. I hope we can work through this."

I shrug Mr. Porter's hands from my shoulders and respond strongly, "Lee has moved on with his life. He's doing fine and there should not be a problem."

Mr. Porter waddles quickly behind his desk and takes a seat in his high-back chair. "Well that's what I want to talk about – Lee not being a problem. It seems that Lee took a disk of company information. You wouldn't happen to know anything about that, would you Diane?" Mr. Porter asks nervously.

"No," I answer uneasily.

I remember Lee saying he had something on the company, but I thought he was just crazy and venting. Mr. Porter sits back in his chair and stares at me as if there's something more he's waiting for me to say.

"Will there be anything else, Mr. Porter?"

"As a matter of fact there is, Diane. I need that disk. Can you call Lee and ask him about it?" he asks, leaning forward with his fat arms on his desk.

"Now?"

"Now."

"Why is it so urgent that I talk to Lee, Mr. Porter?"

"Well, let's just say he's violated company policy. A theft of company property would be the case here, Diane, and I would like to avoid getting the authorities involved."

"Lee is an honest man, Mr. Porter. He would not steal from the company. You must be mistaken!"

142

Mr. Porter stands abruptly, knocking his chair to the floor. "Listen here, damn it! That bastard has that computer disk. You get his ass on the phone now, or there'll be hell to pay!" Mr. Porter bellows.

I am startled by his outburst and realize that Lee must have something that could damage this man. I recall Lee saying something about double books at the house. Maybe Mr. Porter is the thief. Trying and remain calm because I have no idea where Lee could be, I decide to call home to pacify the obviously deranged Mr. Porter. The phone rings twice and my heart skips a beat when Lee picks up.

"Hello".

"Lee, I'm in Mr. Porter's office and ..." Mr. Porter snatches the phone from me and turns on the speakerphone.

"Look you bastard, you bring me my god damned disk or I'm blowing your wife's brains all over my office. You must not know who you're fucking with!" Mr. Porter screams as he reaches into his desk, retrieves and aims a .38 revolver at me.

Lee's voice came through crystal clear and cold as ice, when he said, "I told you I'd get you back, didn't I, Porter? You were setting up foreign accounts, robbing the company blind. Then you planned to just disappear, like you have in the past. I checked up on you Mr. Porter, or shall I call you by your real name, Mr. Reynolds?"

"Don't worry about my name, asshole. You worry about your pretty little wife here staying alive. You bring me the disk in one hour or me and Diane are gonna get sexy and then she's gonna get dead!"

I swallow hard and feel bad that I didn't believe in Lee and support him. I pray that he will get here in time so I won't be harmed. Mr. Porter, or whatever this man's name was, walks over to me and cups my breasts as he places the revolver to my head. He pushes my legs apart and presses his hand inside my panties, strokes my vagina, then places his fingers to his nose and breathes in deeply. Porter grins wickedly and says, "Mr. Lee, take your time. I think I'll start that party now, asshole!"

I close my eyes and shut my legs, feeling violated. I'd rather die than give in to his desires.

"Mr. Reynolds, walk over to the window!" Lee demands.

Mr. Reynolds inquires, "What the hell for?"

"If you want the disk, go to the window," Lee directs angrily.

Mr. Reynolds hesitantly goes to the window. "Now what?" he asks smugly.

"Look across from you at the top of the building."

When we look up, there is a SWAT team of snipers with direct aim at him. Infra red laser dots scatter the front of his shirt in red dots. Mr. Reynolds has been targeted. The door bursts open and five men wearing FBI bulletproof vests rush through the door with guns drawn. Lee is one of the five. He bolts for Mr. Reynolds, snatches his gun and knocks him to the floor with a powerful blow to his jaw. The other FBI agents pull Lee off of him.

"Don't you ever lay your filthy hands on my wife again!" Lee screams, pointing at the cowering man. I run to Lee embarrassed, scared and confused.

"Baby, I'm sorry for this. I'll explain everything on the way home. Let me wrap this up." Lee asks as he hugs me tight, kisses me on the lips and walks me over to a lady FBI agent who brings me into another part of the building and makes sure I'm safe.

It's been a week since the incident and I lay in Lee's arm naked and flushed from the lovemaking we've just enjoyed. Lee has been working under cover for the FBI when Top Investors started getting nervous about the drop in dividends with the company and the possibility that funds were being diverted to overseas accounts. Lee was sent in to investigate and infiltrate the company. He hadn't planned on getting involved with me and for a while thought I was in on the ploy to steal money from the company, but found out soon I knew nothing about it. I made him pay for his suspicions about me by taking me away for the weekend to Belize. We made love under waterfalls and skinny-dipped in the ocean at night. We both needed time to gather ourselves and romantically entwine our devotion. Now I lay in my man's arms, happy in life, happy in the security of trust and romantically in love.

Dallas Deportment

Dallas Deportment (Behavior)

It was a warm, rainy, dreary night when I arrived in Dallas from a two-hour flight from Kansas City delayed because of the storms that swept the Midwest and dirty south. It was all worth it when I saw my baby, Indigo waiting for me in baggage claim. She was so fine and voluptuous in jeans that clung low revealing her shapely waist and belly button. Her white button down top clung to her body and revealed her beautiful dark skinned cleavage, as her nipples seemed to raise and say hello to me.

I embraced her feeling the moisture from the Dallas heat that had kissed her before me. It left a scent of Dallas dew on her skin that turned me on, as her temptress perfume embraced me with its mystical essence.

"I have a surprise for you at the hotel. I know you're stressed from the long flight so I've planned a quiet evening so that we could enjoy the storm," she whispered in my ear as she squeezed my ass.

When we climbed into her black SUV with tinted glass. She reached over and grabbed me between the legs and pulled me to her kissing me like she had really missed me. It had been a month since I was in Dallas.

"So why the hotel baby? Your house is fine," I ask as she pulls onto the I-35 Highway.

She turned and winked at me, "baby, you know I live in Plano and that's thirty minutes that I could have you all to myself instead of us on the road driving. I'm still one hour and a half behind of filling you up with my love. Baby, I got to make up for lost time, while you sat on the runway in Kansas City. I got to make that time up baby. I hope you took a nap on the plane cause you're gonna need your stamina tonight, Indigo replied with a devilish grin.

I looked her up and down and started to play with her neck and her locks that fell below her shoulders and she moaned from the fingertip massage. The rain had subsided for the moment and I saw that she was enjoying the damp Dallas air as the wind from her partly open sunroof let in the warm breeze as the air conditioner blew in the cool. I let my fingers roam to her breast as the moaning increased, then to her nipples. She swerved the car on the slick road and I stopped.

"Damn baby, it will be fucked up if we died before I got to make love to you and I'd hate to die with a frown on my face and my dick hard." We both laughed.

"Okay baby, but we only have a few more miles to go and that shit felt good so, don't stop. I love the way you touch me."

Indigo seemed to have more control of the truck now, so I reached over and kissed her neck as I unfastened her pants. I peeled the zipper and let my fingers creep into her thong and roam between her legs to find her wet secret place. She bit her lip as I massaged her erect clit between my thumb and index finger.

Indigo moaned in ecstasy and as her moans became louder, her legs started to shake. "That's it, daddy, right there. That's my spot. Oooh Blake, that shit ain't right, but it's s damn good," she said as she pulled into the parking lot of the Ritz Carlton Hotel. She leaned over and kissed me passionately again. We got out of the car, got my suit bag and we entered the hotel and taking the elevator to the 29th-floor suite enjoying every minute of the ride.

I sat down my leather suit bag and watched Indigo sashay around the spacious room lighting candles she had strategically placed around the suite before turning the lights of She opens the French doors to welcome the lightning from the thunderstorm set the moo and was a perfect backdrop for our twilight serenade. The illumination of the jasmir scented candles, along with breeze flows through the room creating a scene of enchantmer and ambiance.

Indigo comes to me peering deep into my eyes, while unbuttoning my Italian crushed si shirt and lets it fall to the floor. She offers me her tongue as she grips my hairy chest and unbutton her top as well and feel her firm breast against my skin. We simultaneousl unfasten each other's pants and she pulls them down along with my boxers and I step out c them. She reaches down and strokes my bulging erection. I slowly undress her and kis her body from head to her ankles. The air from the storm blows through the open Frenc balcony doors and caresses our naked bodies. The candles flicker as shadows danc sensually across the walls of the room.

"Just An Illusion," the Najee CD is playing as we dance to the rain that has quickly begu to downpour. The music fills our souls as we flow with it. The touch and smell of her sk is mesmerizing. We tenderly caress each other's bodies as we keep melodic pace to th slow sexy saxophone that is floating hypnotic notes into the airwaves. I've never been th happy and turned on by a woman's essence and sensuality. My baby is so jazzy.

"I missed you, Indigo. After the game all the players be getting with the gold diggers that wait for us at the hotel trying to give up the pussy, but I just walk away baby, cause no overnight sex thing can get close to this. You fill me up and it's always worth the wait. Shit you turn me on! I feel like I can cut diamonds right now, my dick is so hard," I whisper in my woman's ear.

Indigo giggles as she places her lips next to my ear, "you better not be giving my loving away and don't be wasting all that big dick cutting diamonds when I got the ebony gold mine you can be cutting into."

I shiver from her jazzy voice, stop dancing, and kiss my baby with all of the

passion that thirty days can build up in a man. She leads me to the balcony out in the rain and we are showered by the storm. She grabs the railing and we look at the city lights of the Dallas skyline in the distance.

"Fuck me from the back, Blake," she invites as I come from behind her and cup her breast as she leans over the terrace.
"Baby, I want to take our time and enjoy every second of this shit. It's been awhile. I'll fuck you, but I'm gonna love you first," I whisper in her ear and kiss the base of her neck.

I wipe the raindrops from my face and separate her long sexy legs. My kisses cascade down her back with the raindrops. She raises her hips to welcome me into her sugar shack. I bend down and look at her shaven black pussy and the pink blossom slowly separates like a rose as my hot tongue tickles, licks, spells her name, and dance up and down, side to side, and back and forth on her folds. My baby loves me licking her from the back and I give my baby what she likes. I blow into her secret passionate spot and rub my fingers on her clit. I insert my index finger into her as her passion opens wider to invite in my second and third finger.

"Ooh Blake, I love it when you eat my pussy and finger fuck me like that." Her voice gets louder with each word as her sensual flower contracts against my fingers and she jerks from orgasmic satisfaction. Her thighs tense and she shivers like she's having mini seizures, then she relaxes and turns her head to look at me as the rain baptizes us in our love.

"Give it to me now, baby," Indigo orders.

I stand up as she grabs my throbbing erect dick and places it inside her wet, welcoming, world. I enter her slowly from behind wanting to savor every inch of my penetration. We get in rhythm with the storm and the Will Downing song that is playing from the CD inside. The rain flows down our bodies as our orgasmic juices follow closely behind the raindrops that puddles at our feet.

I turn her around and kiss her softly as the storms rains consumes us in its wetness.

"Baby, this is so exciting. I couldn't wait for our football team to get a bye so I could come and see you. I needed the rest. Playing defensive back can take it's toll on a brothers nerves and body and we got the playoffs in another three weeks. You got to leave your office more often and come take care of your man. Southern Comfort magazine will survive without you for a day or two."

"Blake, you know I'll be there. Let's go inside, I still have a surprise for you." Indigo says as she leads me back into the suite.

"Baby, I have a surprise for you, too. Let me put my bag in the bedroom and I'll get it for you."

Indigo, pulls me to her and away from the slightly ajar door to the bedroom. "No, you can't go in there. "That's where I'm keeping your surprise. Let's bathe first."

I could have sworn I heard something in there, but maybe it was the thunder. I dismiss it as she leads me to the large bathroom with an oversized Jacuzzi that is large enough for three or four people. I sit on the side of the marble tub drying our bodies as she runs hot, steamy, water for us to continue our erotic evening. She went into the suite and returns with a gallon of milk and honey-almond bubble bath gel. With love, Indigo pours them both into the tub and bubbles immediately erupt into life.

"Damn baby, so the next thing you'll be pouring in the is corn flakes, huh?" I say joking.

Indigo punches me in the arm, "No silly, milk is very good for the skin, and you'll see how good it feels."

The water rises and she slowly turns on the cold water and checks to make sure the temperature is just the way we like it. When the water is about four inches above the jets she turns on the Jacuzzi button. The water swirls and the bubbles rise. We step down into the tub and immerse ourselves into the hot welcoming water. We kiss and fondle each other as the jets blow the hot water against my spine. It feels so good against my sore back muscles.

I quickly think of how I can use the pulsating water to please my woman. I move beneath the water and place Indigo in just the right position where the jets blow the hot bubbly water across her rectum and pussy as I take her succulent breast into my mouth one by one, making sure they each get pleasure from my tender affection. My tongue dances to each erect nipple and I take as much of her titties into my mouth as I can. I commence sucking them, flicking my tongue, then tapping her hard ebony nipples from one side to the other.

Indigo throws her head back and screams in ecstasy as orgasms take hold of her. Her body trembles from the excitement. I love it when she squeezes her eyes shut and grips my forearms to temper her erotic rush of joy and satisfaction.

She looks at me nodding her head and smiling like she can't believe what just happened. She leads me to the step on the bathtub, which exposes my erect penis. It looks like a black Washington Monument, jetting from the white bubble clouds that have formed around my balls. She cups them both with one hand as the other grabs the muscles of my abdomen. She bites my lower lip, and then kisses me letting our hot tongues dance in each other's mouths with wet intoxication. She kisses my chest, working her way to my navel, and then with her tongue she entices the head of my dick, flicking her tongue around the top as her fingers strum my balls and has my dick throbbing and yearning for the warm confines of her mouth, throat, and hot saliva.

My baby doesn't disappoint me as she strokes my dick up and down with her tongue and hand leaving me shaking from excitement. She takes all of me in her mouth and I arch my back from the hot water and bubbles. Her head moves faster up and down keeping melodious rhythm with my heavy breathing and moaning. She starts to deep throat me and jack's me off at the same time. Her firm grip is magnificent. All the excitement within me is smoldering at the tip of my dick as I grab the back of her head and hold a hand full of her beautiful black locks. The smoldering becomes an eruption as I release the sensual volcanic overflow into her mouth. It feels like all the electricity in my body is flowing up and down my spine as my stomach tingles.

"Got damn baby, you trying to kill a brother or what?" She looks at me as she licks the remnants of my satisfaction from my dick that is throbbing from excitement. That shit turns me on.

"Baby, I got all you need right here and I want you to feel the same way you make me feel. I fantasize and relive all our lovemaking escapades in my mind. I bring extra panties to the office just to get me through the day. I think about all we do and I get very wet and excited at the thought and I have to touch myself to stop my pussy from throbbing."

With that I take Indigo into my arms and kiss her with all the confidence and pleasure that she builds inside me. We delve back into the warm water a soap two sponges and wash each other from head to toe, kissing the whole time. We finally rinse and step out of the tub, turn off the jets and dry each other off as we let our fingers explore each other.

I grab the lavender scented massage oil from the stand as I lead her to the king size bed to massage my woman like she needs to be. I lay her down and kiss her before I began. I marvel at her lovely body as I massage the silky oil into my hands, straddle my woman's voluptuous backside and meticulously apply the warm oil to her neck and shoulders. I move to her elbows, arms, wrists, and fingertips.

"How do you like that baby?" I ask as she moans beneath my body.

She turns her head smiling, "Daddy, you know how to spoil a woman. I want you so bad right now.

"Good things comes to those who wait," I whisper in her ear as I move to her ass and oil her buttocks one at a time.

I kiss her ass and take little bites to excite her and make her senses explode with passion. I move to her thighs and gently rub on her pussy to make it tremble between my fingers as I tease her, then move to her legs, ankles and feet. I give great attention to my woman's feet, because that is one of her pleasure points. I take her toes one by one into my mouth and suck on them, letting my tongue dance across them as I recite, "This little piggy, went to the market," she bursts out laughing and I could have swore I heard a giggle coming from the bathroom.
I ignored it and turned my baby over and massaged her shoulders and neck. I Let my fingers creep like large spiders to her firm breasts, stomach, waist and had to taste her sugar shack once more as it invited me with its sensual spell bounding smell. I spread her legs and placed them across my shoulders giving me full access to her sugar. I spelled the alphabet on her pussy and spelled our names out as well with my tongue. I sucked on her clit, then blew air to dry it and started all over until her climactic juices of satisfaction poured down my chin as her thighs jerked and squeezed my neck. I love it when Indigo cum.

"Oh shit baby, you did it now," Indigo purred as she turned me over on my stomach.

She climbed atop my back and whispered in my ear. "Get excited, close your eyes and get ready for this big surprise. You have me feeling hypnotized, the way you went down between my thighs. I want to thank you for being so good to me and wanting to please me constantly, I wanted to share with you my fantasy, and give you my world unconditionally."

She starts massaging the nape of my neck and my shoulders. She works her way up to my baldhead, then back down to my elbows, arms, fingers, then to my back. The oil feels good and her fingers and hands feels even better. I notice her wet pussy on my ass and it excites me. I think I'm going crazy as I notice a pair of hands in my lower back and another set of hands massaging my ass. Either my woman grew another set of hands, or that giggle from the bathroom materialized into another person. I turn and look up at Indigo who looks at me and winks. I look across at the other person who is a gorgeous red boned sister, with a short haircut that's cute. She has a dancer's body that is just as bad as my woman's. She has a Betty Boop tattoo above her right breast and a nipple ring in her left nipple.

Blake, this is Stacy Benoit. She is a college friend of mine from New Orleans, she's moved here to Dallas last month. She's your surprise. She wanted to meet you, so I asked her to join us. So lay back and enjoy baby.

"Your in for the time of your life, Blake," Stacy says with a deep southern accent as she slaps me on the ass.

"I hope y'all are ready for this," I say as I lie down and enjoy the body massage as my mind and dick are both ready to explode from the sexual possibilities. I just love this Dallas deportment, I think to myself.

about the author

Vincent Alexandria - "If Walls Could Talk", "Postal Blues", "Black Rain", & "Poetry from the Bottom of My Heart." (We Must X-L Publishing Co.) He is an author, actor, producer, director, composer, lyricist, vocalist, screen writer, and musician. He is the father of four children. He holds a Masters degree in literature at Baker University and holds a Bachelor's degree in Psychology from Rockhurst College. He's a GED Teacher with the EVENSTART Program in Kansas City, MO. His vision for the Brother 2 Brother Symposium is to enlighten men and women in reading and comprehension to enhance their quality of life. Having nationally published authors show a commitment to their communities and give back to their readers in gratitude of what they have done for them and their careers.